The Mountains of Florida

The Art of Dirt

Take Time To Play In The Dirt!

The Mountains of Florida
The Art of Dirt

by

James A. Harper

DORRANCE PUBLISHING CO., INC.
PITTSBURGH, PENNSYLVANIA 15222

ISBN # 0-8059-5734-0
Printed in the United States of America

First Printing

For information or to order additional books, please write:
Dorrance Publishing Co., Inc.
643 Smithfield Street
Pittsburgh, Pennsylvania 15222
U.S.A.
1-800-788-7654
Or visit our web site and on-line catalog at
www.dorrancepublishing.com

Acknowledgments

Patricia Harper
Tim Neuman
Walter Neuman
Mom & Pop Neuman
Eddie & Fran Norman
Photobition Inc.
Karen & Paul Smith
Dan Laverack

This book is dedicated to my wonderful wife, Patricia. Without your undying love and understanding none of my work would be possible.

James A. Harper can be found on the world wide web at
www.mountainsofflorida.com
E Mail: jph@cfl.rr.com

Introduction

Is there anywhere in the world where mountains aren't special? Especially in Florida, I have found "The Mountains of Florida" in the most unlikely of places. You have driven past them on your way to work, on your way to the beach, and walked past them on your daily exercise walks. The journey I want you to experience through my images of dirt mounds is as much about seeing the world differently as it is about beauty. There is some beauty in everything if you look hard enough for it. Some people see the Virgin Mary or Jesus in puddles of water or oil stains left by automobiles. I see mountain images in piles of dirt and it is my desire to share these images with the world.

Open your imagination and feed your soul the grand illusion of unexplored Florida. My journey has been a ten-year trip in acquiring these images. It is something that I want to share with the world if for no other reason than to spur the imagination. One of our most valuable gifts in this life.

This will not be a "How to" book however, some technical aspects of the dirt that have helped me to create the image of the mountains will be discussed. Why I chose black and white film to portray "The Mountains of Florida" will also be a key discussion as well as the role of the computer in the printing of the final images. It is my hope that the way you view the world will change forever when you close the book. Have you fed your imagination lately?

At one time in everyone's life a mountain has played a role of some sort. They portray strength, inspiration, and solitude. We have climbed to conquer them and leveled them to show our superiority over them. It is where the Ark came to rest. It is where Moses encountered the burning bush. It is where the Ten Commandments were given to Moses. It is where Jesus was tempted by Satan. In some societies it is the center of their existence. The scaling of Mount Everest is still one of the most sought after achievements of mankind. In landscape photography, mountains are the most photographed subject.

Living in Florida, it is very frustrating when I enter contests where I am constantly competing with mountain images for top billing. Don't get me wrong, Florida is very beautiful in many ways and I have created many wonderful images from the landscape. As I stated though, we are drawn to mountains even in the photographic form. One look at the work of Ansel Adams and you can see why. He is one of many masters who have inspired me to look for "The Mountains of Florida."

As a photographer I have always been more drawn to the art side of the image making rather than making stock photos to sell in the market place. I realize that to support myself that it is probably not the best way to go about things. However when you have a feeling in your heart telling you to follow something you had better follow that feeling. As far as I am concerned, the money will come eventually.

Growing up I had a good appreciation for art but nothing on the level of the great masters. My first expression of art was in the form of drawings that were in my imagination. I'm sure if I could look at them now they would be a bit scary. It wasn't until I met my wonderful wife Patricia that my admission of artistic talent could finally come out and play. She has taught me how to express and channel the imagination process.

At the beginning of my artistic journey, we took a trip to Sarasota, Florida, to see the John Ringling art museum. He was a great lover of art as well as a circus owner and his collection includes the famous Rubens paintings. It was awe-inspiring to see the art for the first time. Painting though did not seem to be the medium which I felt I could express my feelings. Once I held our first camera, the excitement of putting images on film felt so natural that I began to pursue fine art photography. I read as much as I could and went to as many seminars as I could to study this art form. One photographer in particular, John Hedgecoe, seemed to write books that I understood and I read his lessons many times. He is an outstanding author as well as photographer. If you can apply the lessons, the results are incredible.

In one of Hedgecoe's books I read a chapter on "Beauty in Strange Places" that seemed to strike a particular chord with me and I began to pursue just that. "If you can't go to the mountains, bring the mountains to you" became my battle cry as I began my search for "The Mountains of Florida." I also began to study the works of the great masters. Ansel Adams, Alfred Stieglitz, and Clyde Butcher were of particular interest. Adams for his mountain images, Stieglitz for his images of clouds at night, and Butcher for his stunning contrast of the black and white Florida landscapes. These masters of the lens would help to shape me as a photographer, to create something that I think you will find to be the next unique original fine art to come around in quite some time.

How many times have you passed by a construction site and been irritated by the dust, noise, and utter chaos? In order for us to advance as a society the building of bigger, better buildings and roads must go on. The very landscape that once gave me joy in one form lay in ruins before me, with the belly of the earth split open before me. I began to frequent these construction sites and places where there was fill dirt piled in excess. I would go at first with no camera just to train my imagination to look for the mountains and in subsequent visits would take the camera to play with angles and shapes.

Sometimes the mountains would not last even a day so I learned to work fast at spotting which dirt would be productive. The first few images were not even close to my expectations, and I toiled over the poor images at first. Suddenly this was becoming a challenge and no longer about winning a contest. My friends began to compare me to

Richard Dreyfuss in the movie Close Encounters. He is told by the aliens to go to the mountain in Utah for an encounter, a mountain that he saw in his mind even before he went there. He even goes so far as to build a replica of it in his living room. I haven't gone that far...yet!

I quickly discovered that in order to get the best images I would have to go out on weekends and holidays when the work crews were not there. Let me state though that whenever possible I would ask permission and make every attempt to contact the foreman. I wanted to be up front about my business with the land owners. To my surprise almost everyone I have met through the course of this project has been very receptive to my wishes. One foreman even said to me "Heck, man, dirt is my business, I think it's beautiful, too. I wanna see it when you're done." I have tried to collect as many business cards as possible in order to do just that.

I wonder as I am creating the images, watching the work crews as they go about their business, if they even know that they are helping me to create "The Mountains of Florida." Have they seen what I have seen in the now seemingly dead landscape? Do they know that from the death of the land there will come life or are they just too busy to do anything about such thoughts?

I never alter the dirt mounds in any way. This is a non-negotiable rule. I make no attempt to move things or put fake snow on them. It must be entirely as found, just as natural mountains—formed only by the wind and rain as real mountains are. Many times people have suggested to me that I put snow from a can on a particular mountain as if that would make the image complete. I say the image is complete when I close the shutter on the natural dirt mound. This standard of creating the image is the art of what I do.

It takes a lot of patience and a very open minded approach to see mountains in the devastated landscape. Not obvious at first glance however, you must challenge yourself to look deeper for the image.

My images have been compared to Ansel Adams's work far too often, and I have mixed emotions about this comparison. I could never attain the quality of work that the master was able to attain. On the other hand, I am flattered by the comparison. The only real comparison is that we both chose to create mountain images and we both used black and white film to do so.

Adams had no real choice of film; however, I do have a choice. I am frequently asked why I chose the black and white medium as opposed to a color medium. For me the answer was an easy and obvious one. I knew what it was that I wanted to portray through my images. First I can see the final image in black and white as I am looking through the lens. That helps when you are creating two–tone images. Secondly in color images your eye is drawn away from the subject and straight to the color. I do not want any distractions such as this to draw the viewers's eyes away from the subject matter. Next is the contrast that I get with the black and white film. I need the contrast to emphasize the canyons and crevices that give the mountains the appearance of natural mountains. The contrast simply will not translate properly onto color film. The contrast in the clouds that helps put scale into the image is also very important.

It takes a very special pile of dirt to create a mountain without clouds that looks natural. The clouds are very important to the image and black and white film is the best choice for the contrast needed. Another reason also deals with effect. What appears to be snow on the mountains is actually sand that will only translate properly in black and white. If I am fortunate enough to have clouds, snow, and a mountain that has great contrasting crevices all in one scene, it really shows off all of the qualities the black and white film has to offer. It is rare that I have all of these conditions present at once and those images that I have with the whole index of conditions in, I value highly.

The final reason is that I feel closer to the great masters of photography when I am working with my images. I feel a certain sense of duty to create in black and white as a lasting tribute to the great masters who paved the way for me to create art in the photographic form.

It would be unfair to photograph the dirt mounds as mountains and not discuss the dirt itself. I do not want to stray too far outside the subject of making mountain images and turn this into a gardening lesson; however, the dirt that helps me to create the art is very important. I needed to find out the composition that makes up Florida soil for this segment in order to categorize the mountains by soil types. As you will see by the images, some soils photograph better than others. Some soils take on the look of a Midwest mountain. Some look as if they could be in the badlands of Arizona. Some look as if they are part of the Grand Tetons. I have even had some comments that they look like the mountains in Tibet. It takes all different types of soil and lighting conditions to create these different regional appearances.

My starting point for identification was the Florida Department of Agriculture. Gene Fults, who has worked with Florida soil for over forty-five years shared much of the information in this section. Around the time of the last great Ice Age Florida was under water, when the water receded the top soil that was left behind by the oceans was comprised of mostly sand and crushed shell. The top layer of sand is useless in making "The Mountains of Florida." The sand has very little shape and color and contrast when viewed alone and therefore it is unphotogenic.

The sand layer goes down only a few feet and then the layer that is most important is found. The Spodic layer is between ten and forty feet below ground level and is the most plentiful of Florida dirt. That is why it is the most frequently used dirt in my images. I have to frequent the construction sites because the construction crews have brought this important dirt to the surface. Trees, plants, and other forms of life have been broken down over time to form the rich black dirt. The best Spodic dirt for creating the images is found away from the wetland areas. Here it takes on lighter colors with touches of dark soil that help to give it the variances of different rock formations as found in natural mountains. This gives the appearance of mountains that could date back to the dinosaur age.

Close to the wetlands the soil is much too dark to give the contrast needed and exposure is far too difficult with the element of sky being added. Also wetland Spodic contains too many trees and plants remaining in the mounds which would have to be cleared before making the image. This would violate my primary rule of making the mountain images: never alter the dirt from the way it was found. Nothing is fake and nothing is staged. Mountains are natural works of art and so are mine. That is why I get excited when the scene has white sugar sand sitting atop the rich black dirt. I cannot always have snow–covered mountains, but not all natural mountains are snow–covered.

The next layer of dirt in the ground of Florida is the Iron Ore layer. It is a very hard clay-like soil that photographs very well. It takes on the appearance of the Grand Canyon especially when left to sit alone piled up on the surface for a long period of time in the wind, rain, and sun. The crevices become very pronounced and the contrast needed for depth in the image are the factors needed to portray these as Midwest mountains.

The last type of soil that form "The Mountains of Florida" is Mason Sand. It is only found at construction sites. The sand, which is used to mix mortar for brick walls, requires a very special kind of sky and light for a successful image. When I am fortunate enough to find a large pile of the sand I must work quickly to capture the image because the workers use it so quickly. They usually dig out one side of the pile at a time and that is the preferred side to film. When the conditions are ideal, the image is that of an entire mountain covered in snow with huge ice canyons and maybe an avalanche has made an appearance. It is a most stunning image and I wish I had more of them in my collection. The rarity of them, however, makes them very special indeed.

Another important element in the images is the sky. If the sky is not just right I cannot portray the dirt mounds as mountains. I cannot begin to tell you how many times I have had dirt mounds to film and no sky to help complete the image. It is worth passing up beautiful mounds and fantastic light due to a less than desirable sky. That is just how important they are. The ideal sky is when there are a lot of cumulus clouds with high cirrus clouds above them just peeking in between the cotton ball formations. This is very important to give the final image the scale needed. If no clouds are present then the sky must be completely free of any pollution and brilliant blue. The contrast given in this condition is outstanding; however, it does take a very special mound of dirt to portray mountains in a featureless sky.

The element of size is in many ways one of the most important parts of the final image. When people see the image for the first time and are told what it really is, it is an automatic assumption that I was standing in front of a 50 foot pile of dirt. That is where the real story of the art begins. It is very rare to find a huge pile of dirt that will photograph well, so most of the time I am laying on my stomach, my back, or kneeling down. Over time I have found that the best dirt piles are in the two to five-foot high range. There is no real challenge in a huge pile of dirt that has no character. I like the challenge of the smaller mounds and it is always fun to watch the viewer's reactions when they are told it is a three-foot pile of dirt they are looking at. To give an example, "The Mountains of Florida" number one is three feet tall and I was laying on my back when I photographed it. The clouds were perfect in this image and played a major role in the portrayal of the Grand Tetons look.

As far as giving the images names, I am simply not inspired to give them names and I feel that numbers will do the job of identification. I have only been inspired to give one series a name so far. Some were photographed where a church now stands so the name God's Property was given in addition to the numbers. I have debated about naming all of them after the building that now occupies the land, but unfortunately the names just do not always work.

The final element to be discussed is a raging debate in the photography and art world: digital prints versus conventional prints. There are as many arguments for as against. Each artist has to decide for him or herself how to approach the usage of each. If you remember my primary rule for making "The Mountains of Florida" (never alter the natural dirt mounds) then you can see clearly my internal debate. First of all let me say that I am a purist at heart when it comes to making images and do not own a digital camera. There is a certain challenge I enjoy in making the image on a piece of film rather than a computer chip that has an infinite amount of room for alterations.

On the other hand the computer in combination with today's photo programs have brought the digital darkroom into being. Now you are able to scan in your film or prints to be adjusted to your specifications and even remove parts of the image—no chemicals to mess with and no darkroom environment. It would be very tempting to remove some stray branches or leaves from the dirt mounds in order to get a clean image. I cannot be dishonest and feel good about anyone who may view it as pure. I have explored the possibilities though, and it fascinates me. All of the images in this book have been scanned in and printed but not for the purpose of making changes. It is simply easier for me to control the printing process this way. Is this a modern-day darkroom? Is there room for both conventional and digital prints in the world?

Ansel Adams would sometimes spend eight hours at a time in the darkroom adjusting the tones in his images. Today the darkroom has changed its look, but the techniques are the same. I often wonder what advice Adams and Stieglitz would give me in dealing with the transition from conventional to digital. My own solution has been to satisfy the curious animal in me and create a digital print just to see what the possibilities are. "Mountains of Florida #5" has been inverted through the photo program so the white and black parts of the image are reversed. I have also included the original print in the book for comparison. You be the judge.

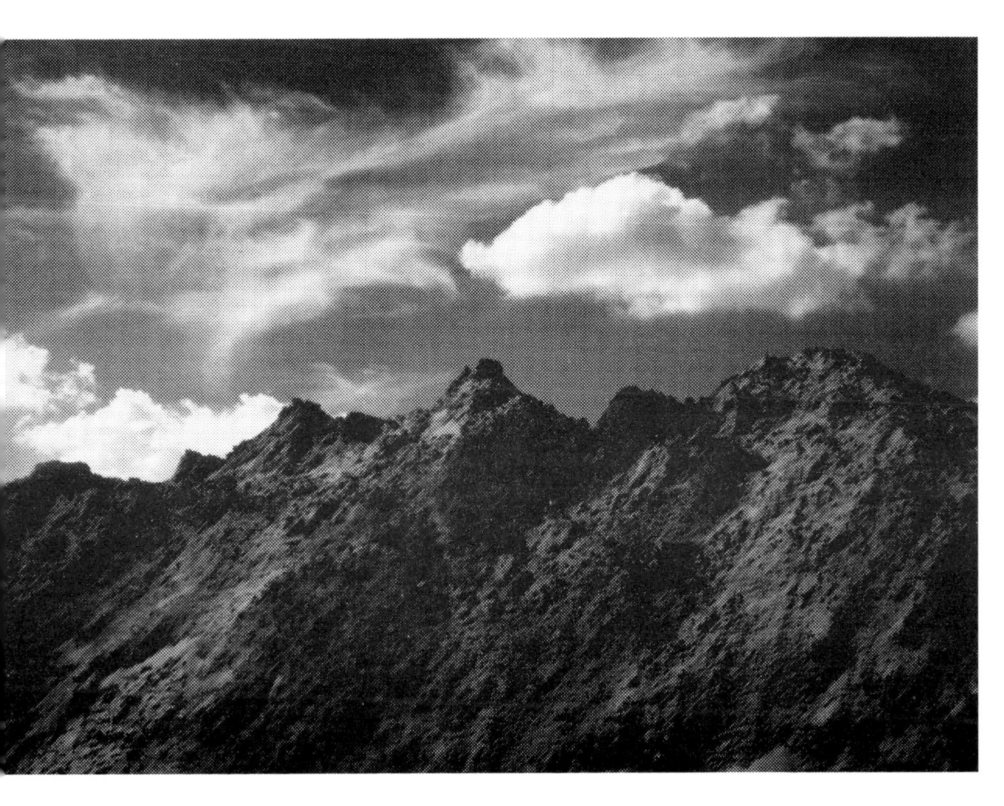

Mountains of Florida I

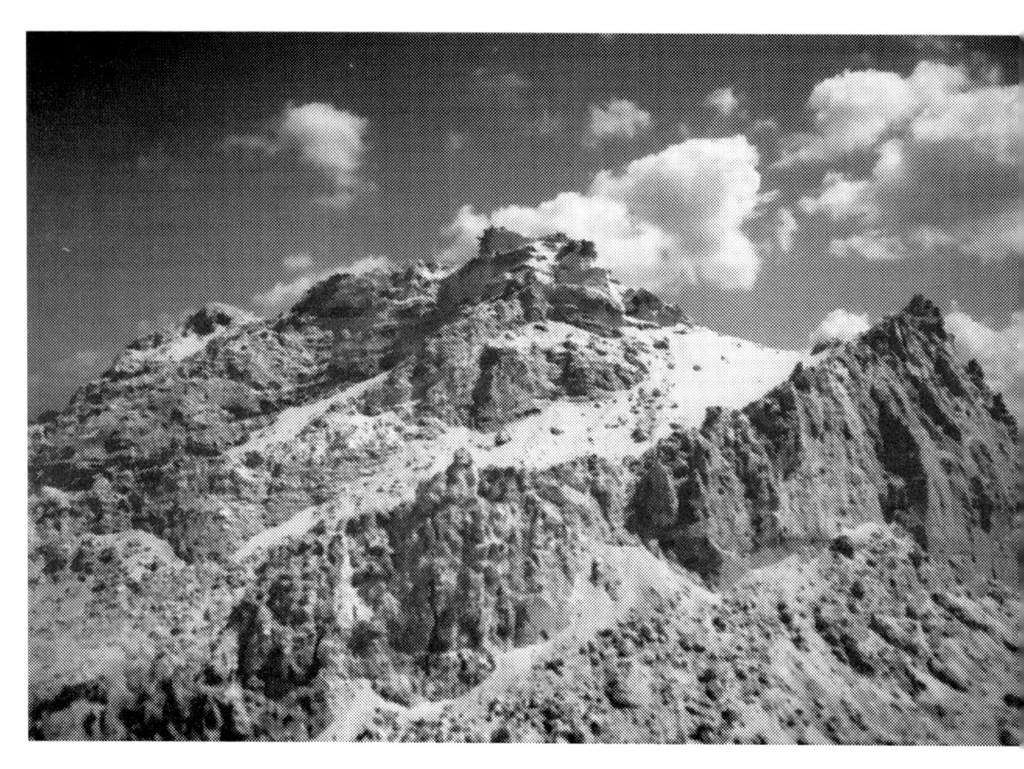

Mountains of Florida II

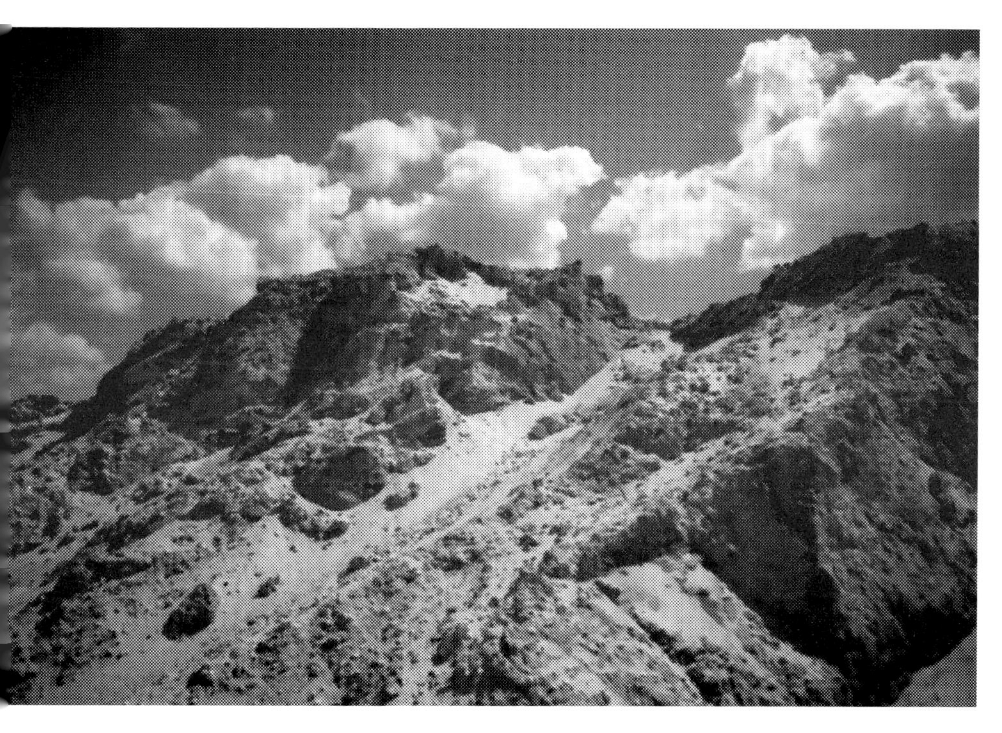

Mountains of Florida III

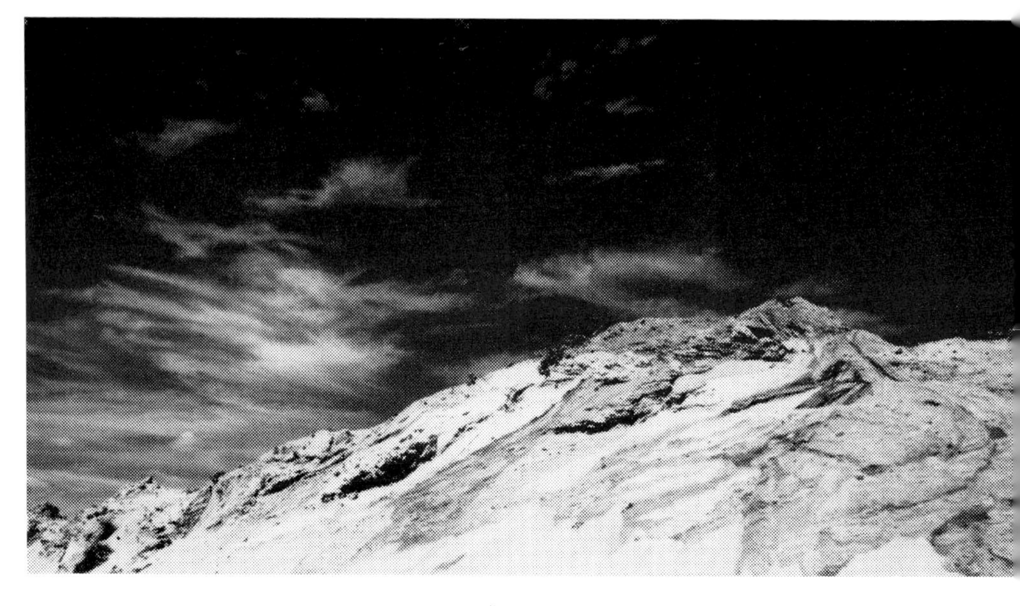

Mountains of Florida IV

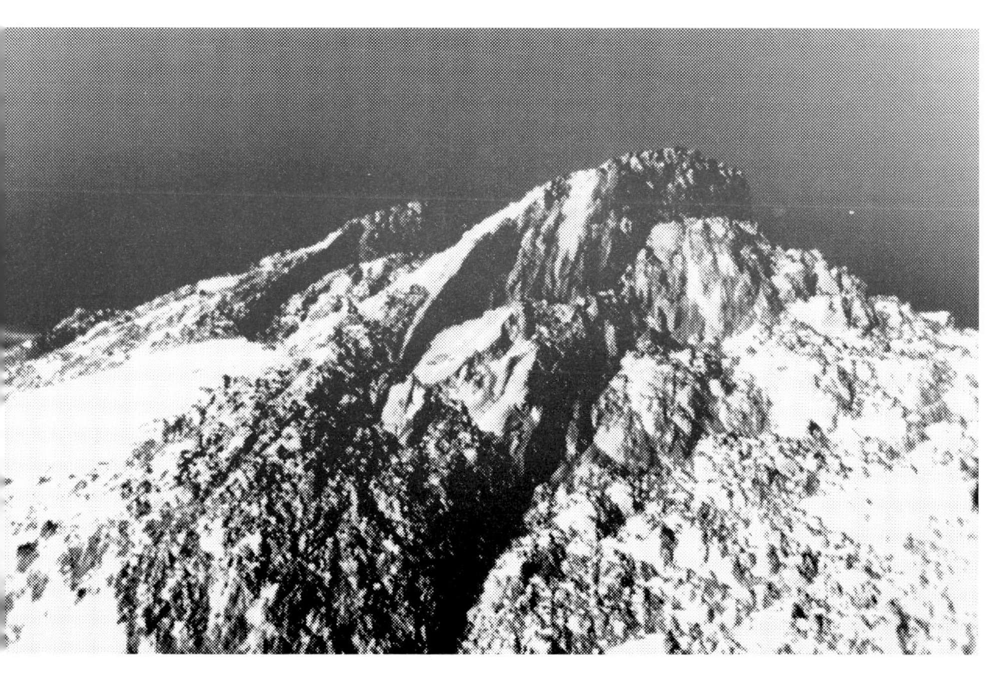

Mountains of Florida V

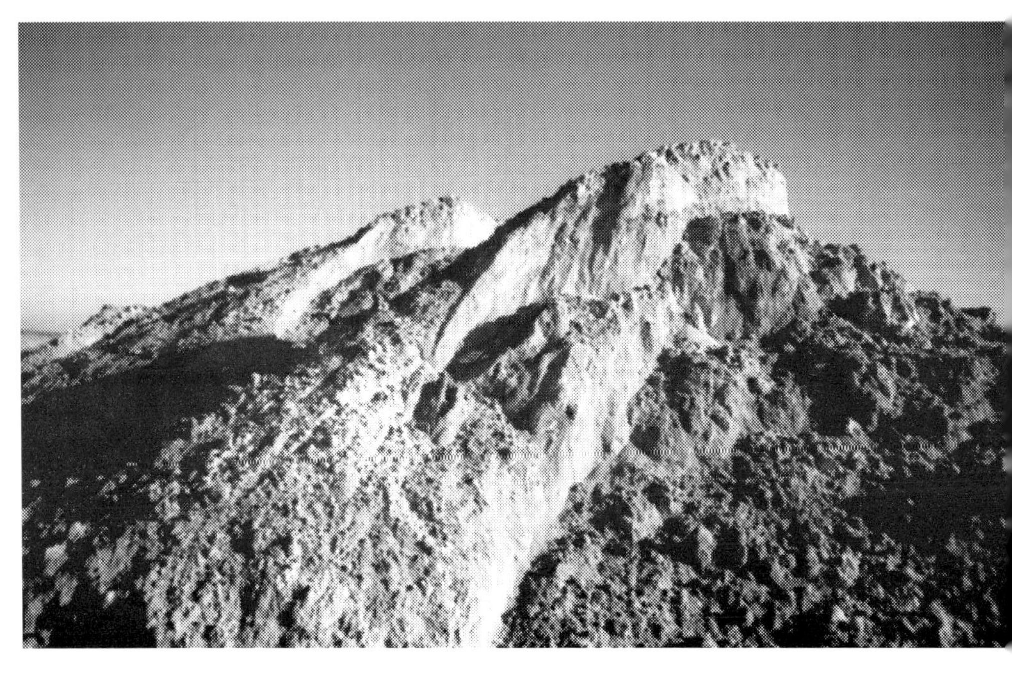

Mountains of Florida VI

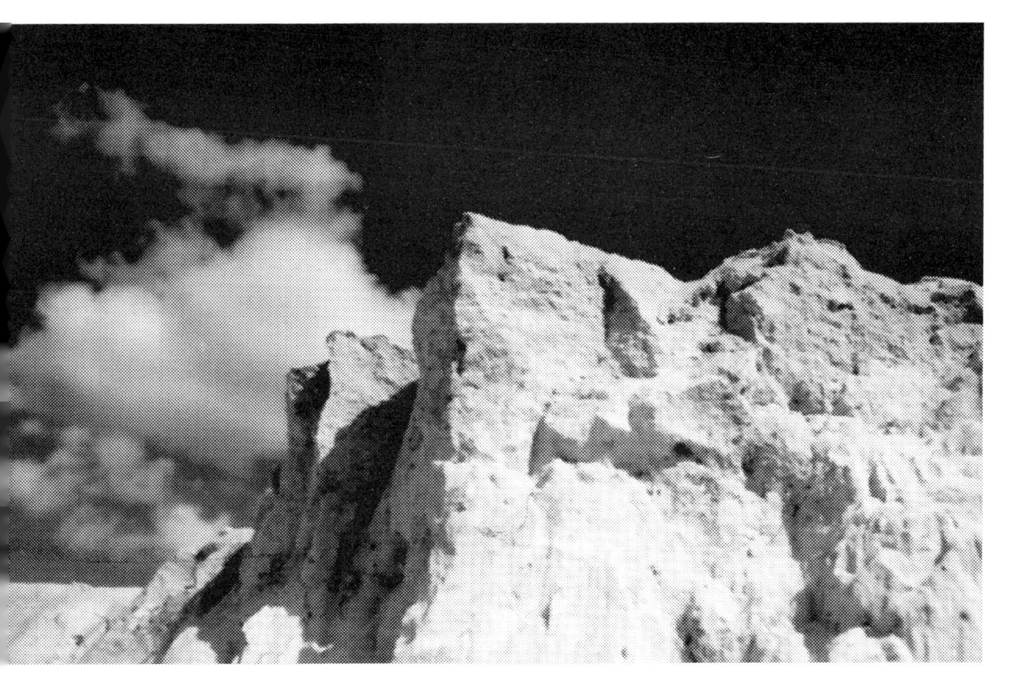

Mountains of Florida VII

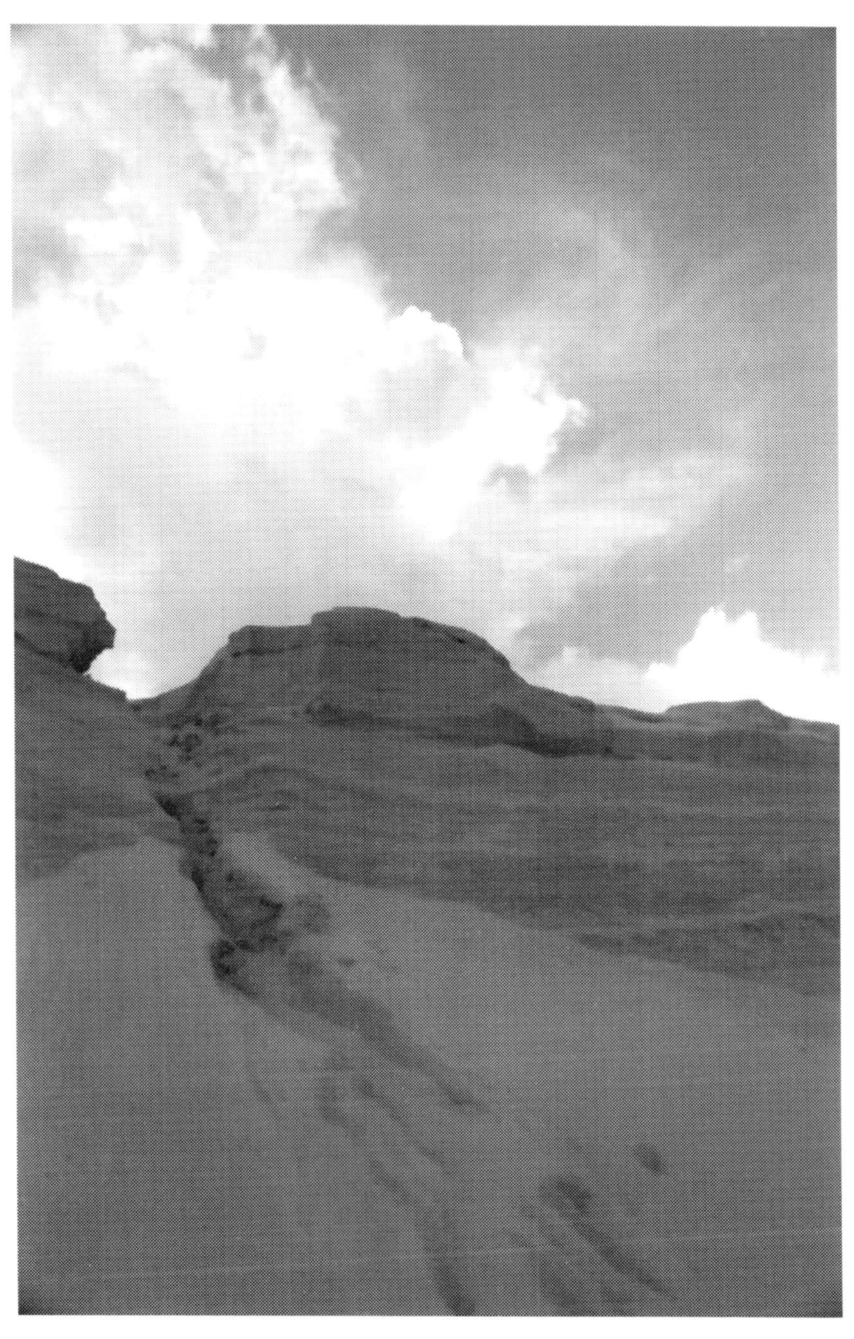

Mountains of Florida VIII

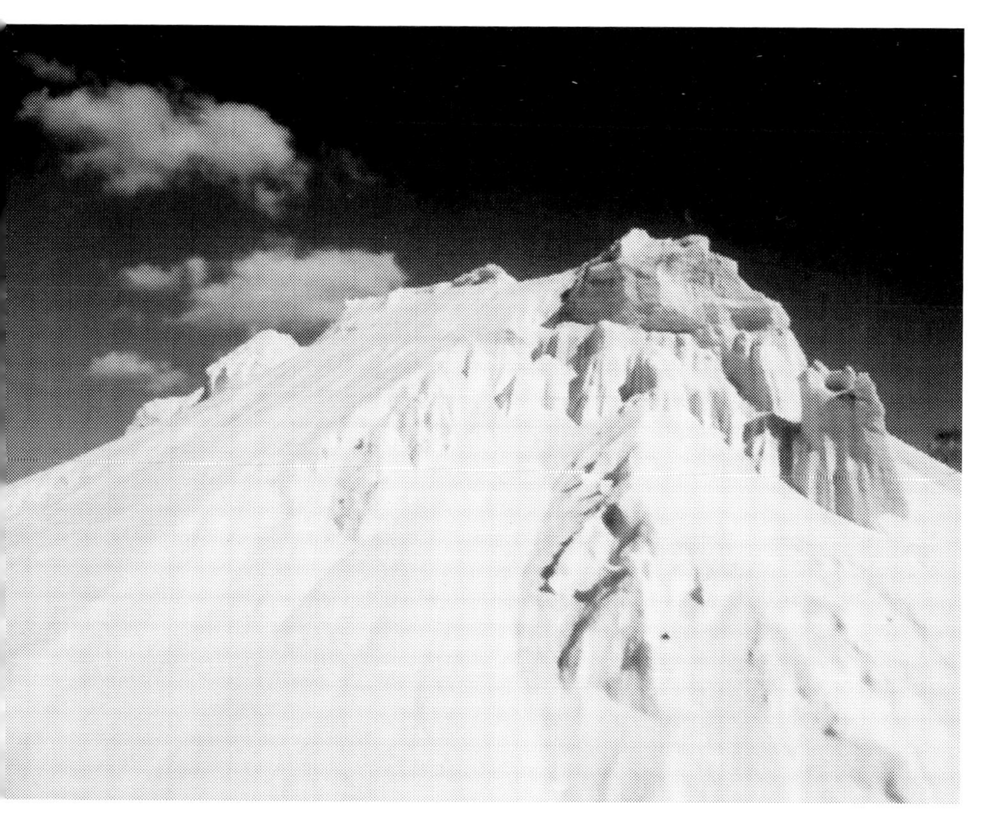

Mountains of Florida IX

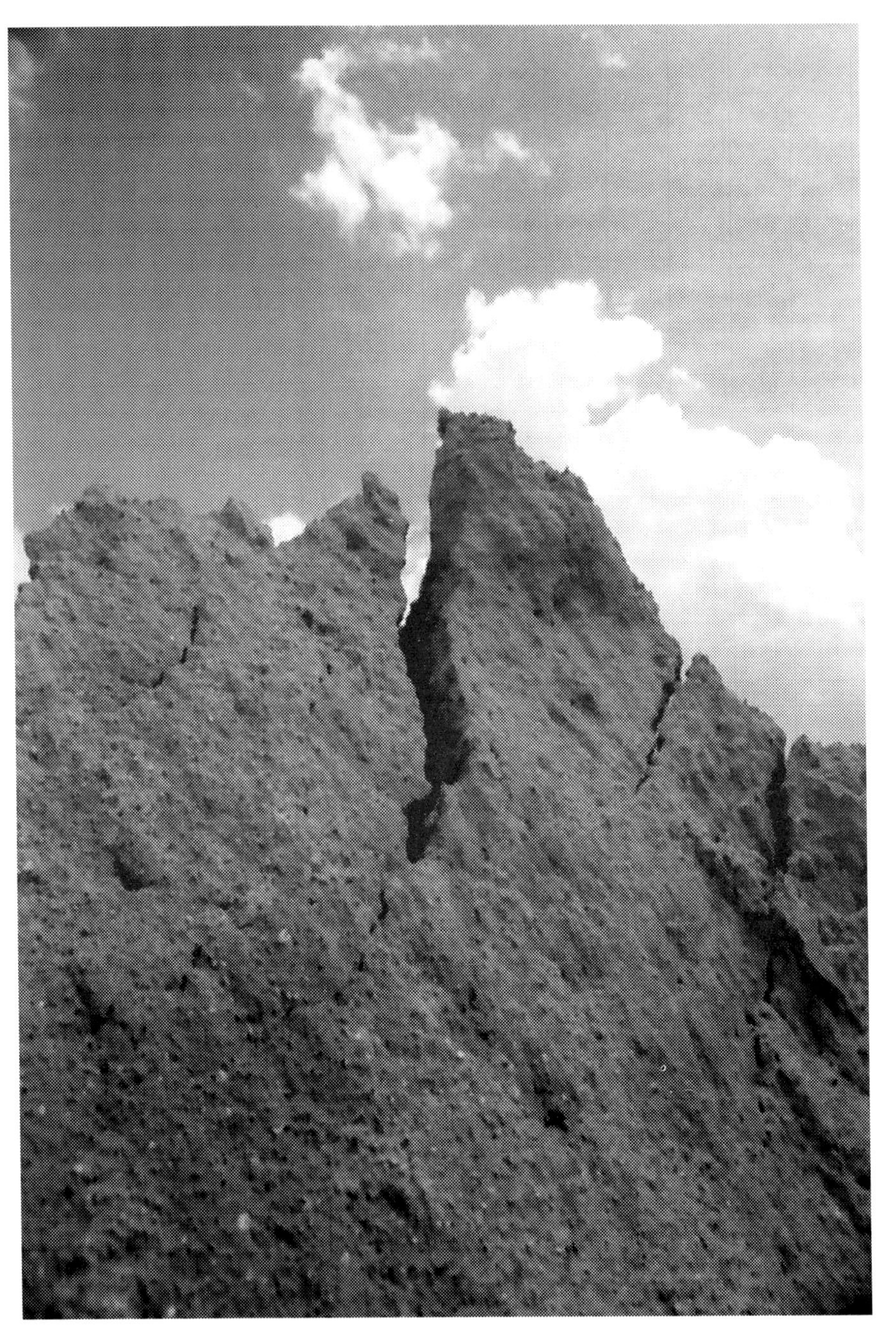

Mountains of Florida X

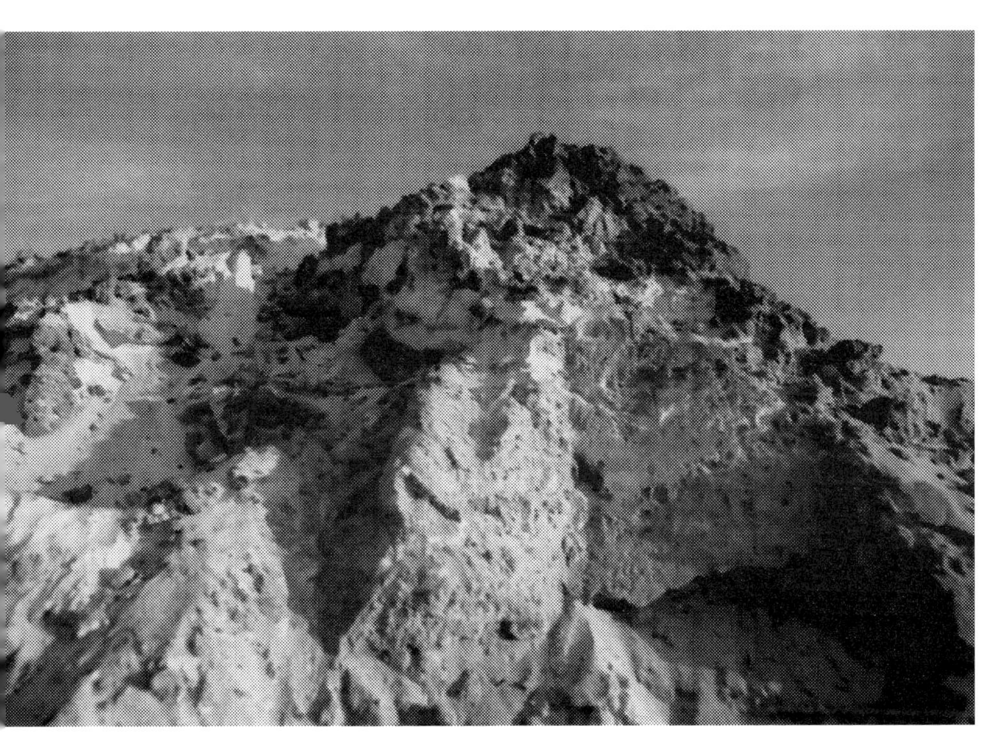

Mountains of Florida XI
Gods Property I

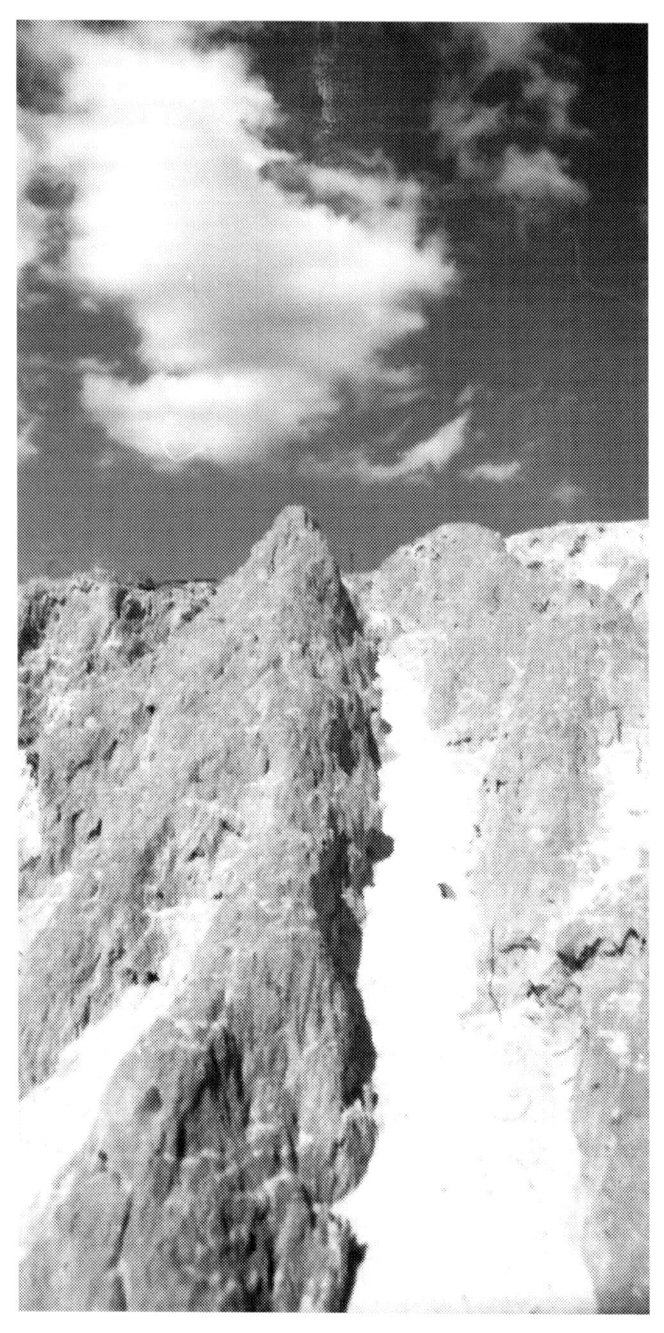

Mountains of Florida XII

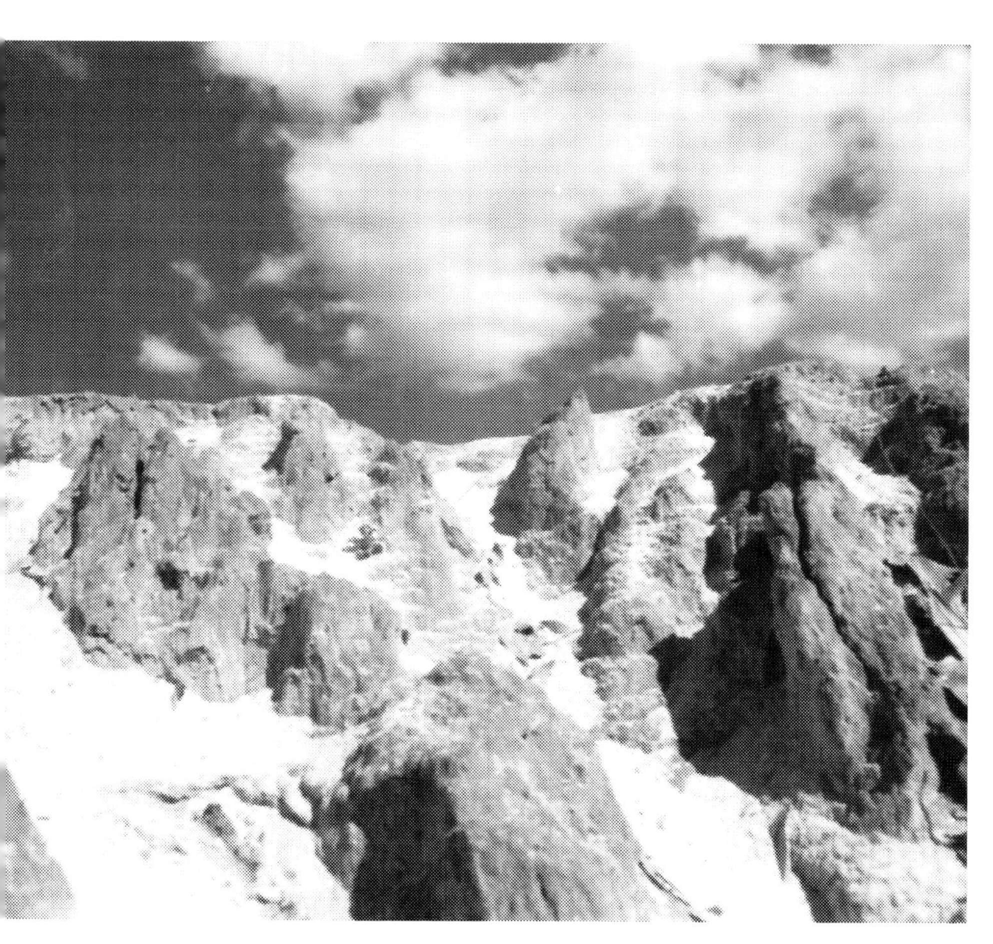

Mountains of Florida XIII

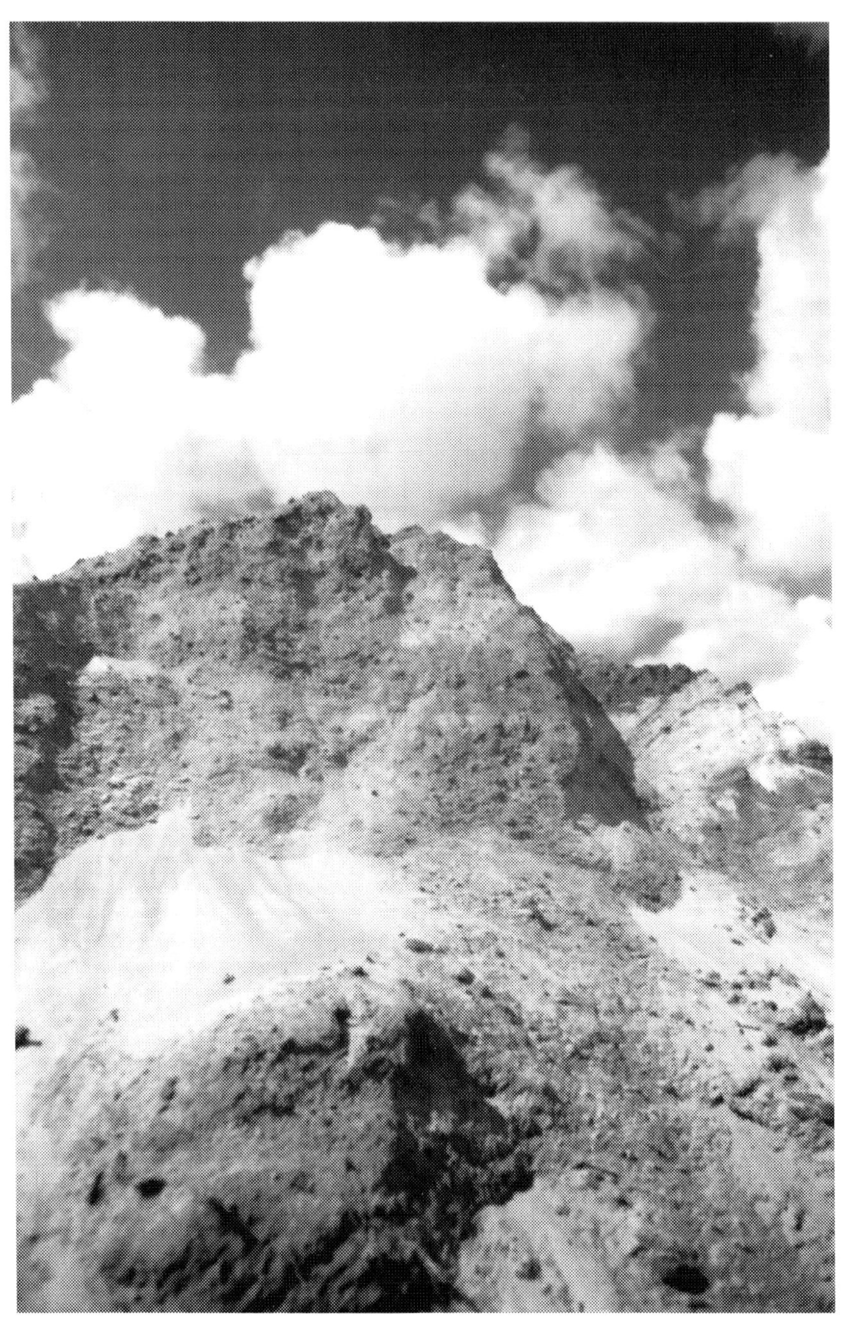

Mountains of Florida XIV

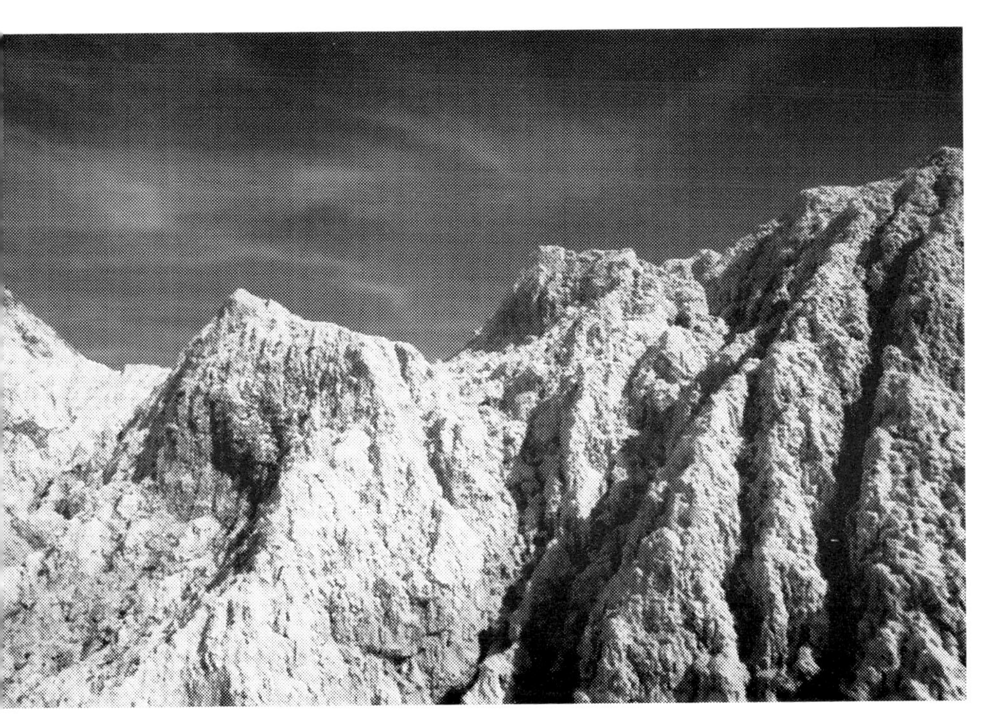

Mountains of Florida XV

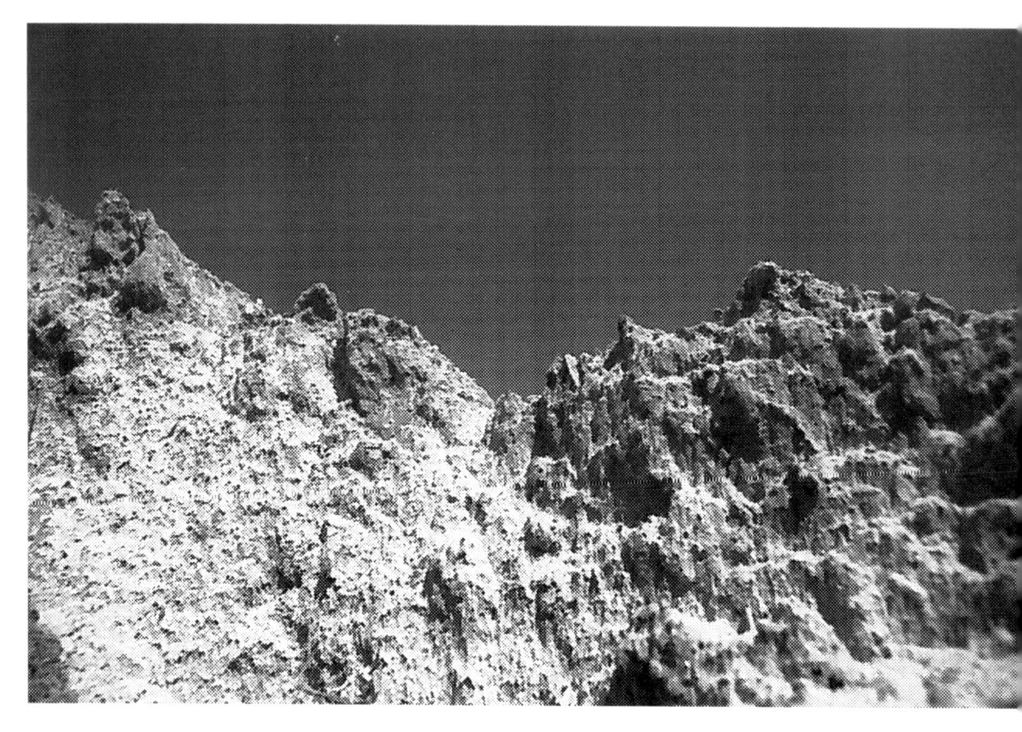

Mountains of Florida XVI
Gods Property II

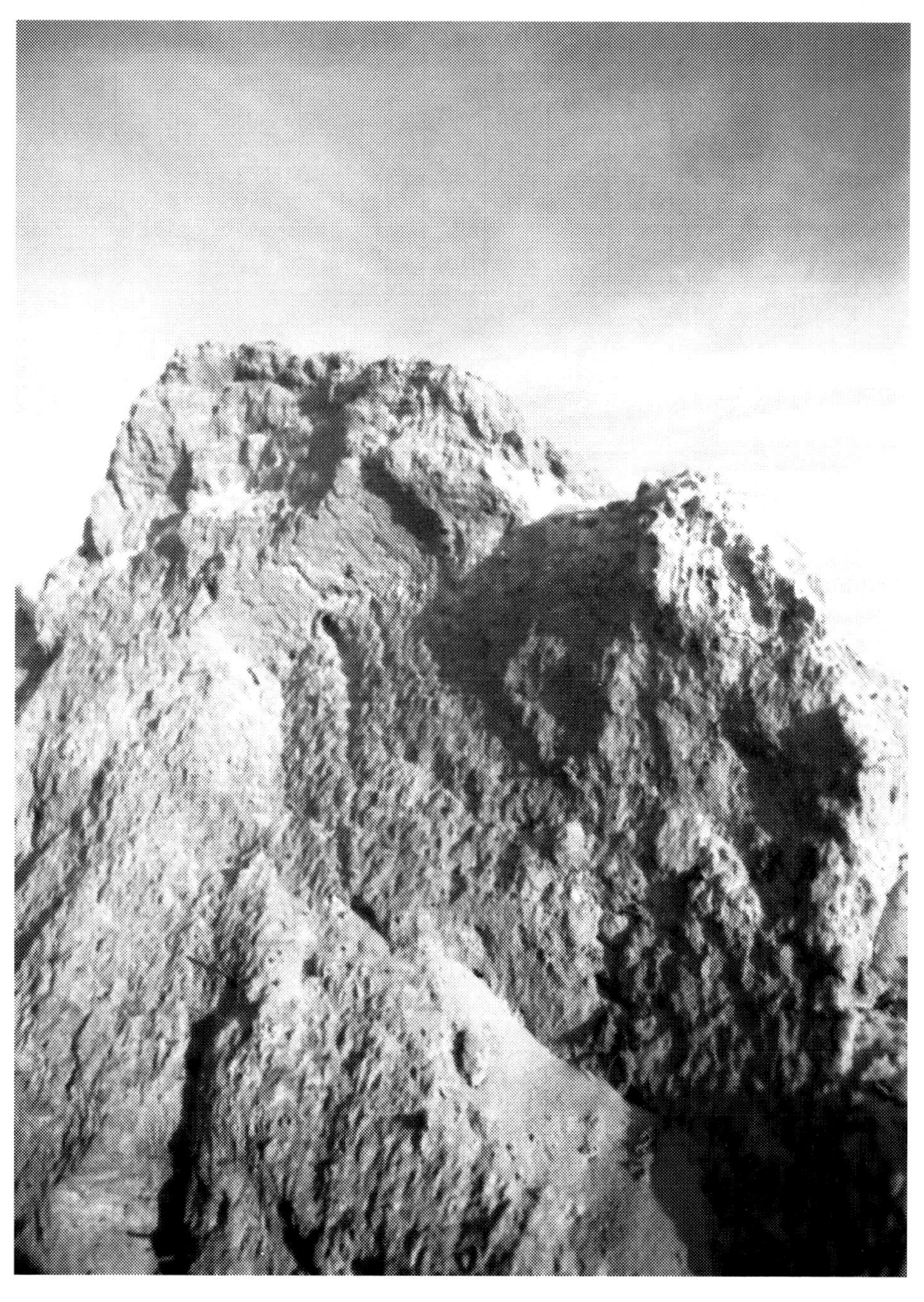

Mountains of Florida XVII
Gods Property III

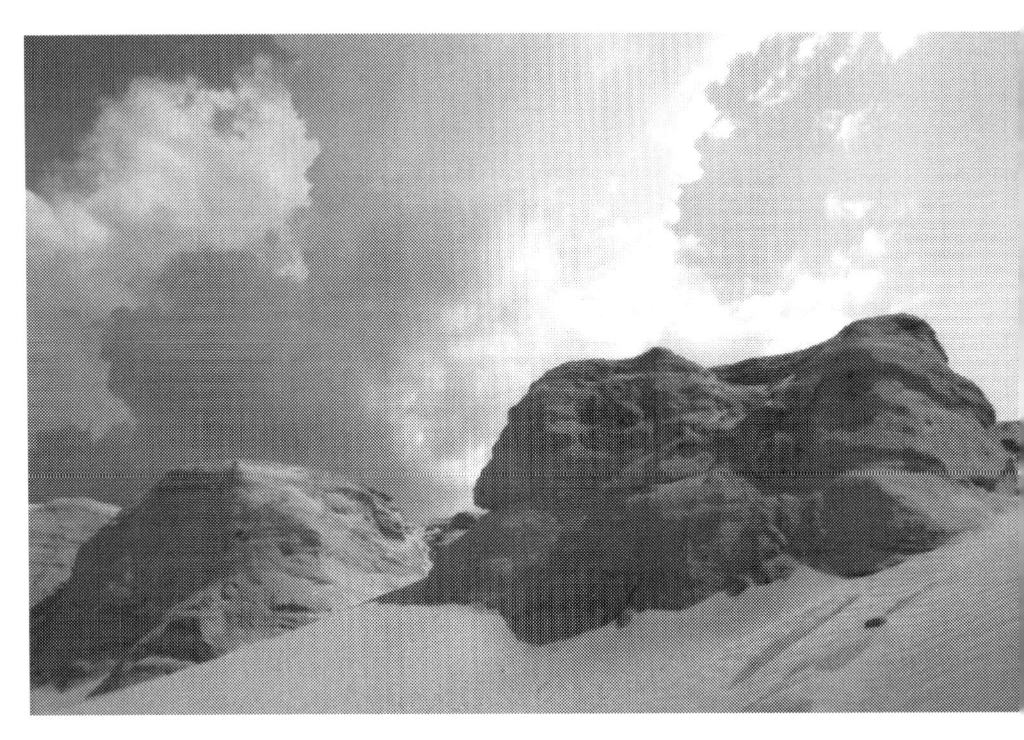

Mountains of Florida XVIII

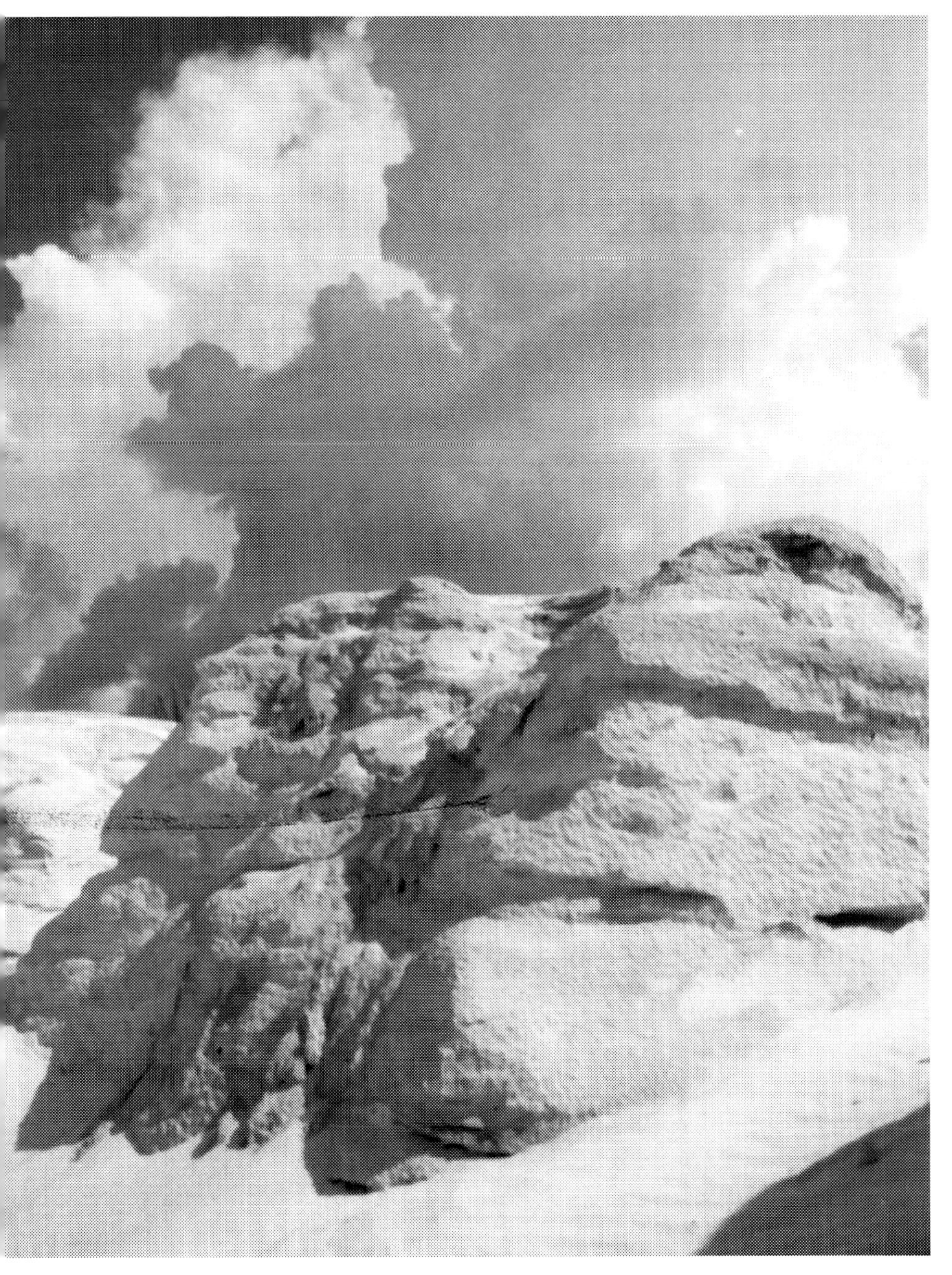

Mountains of Florida XIX

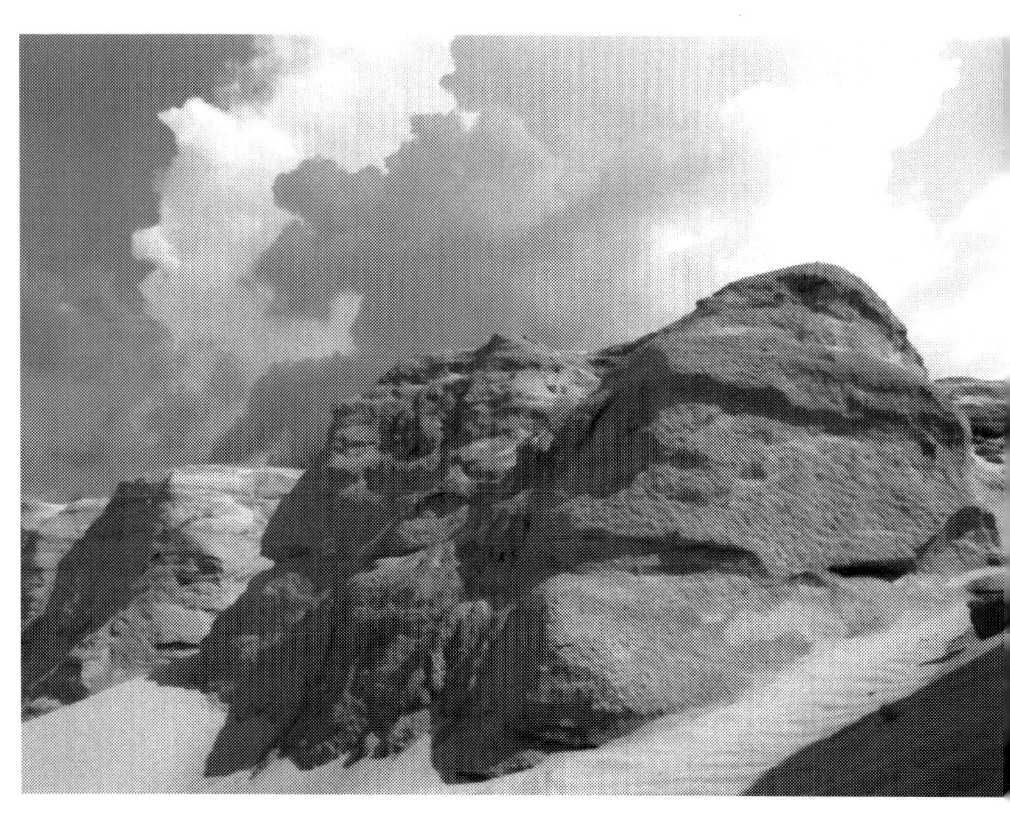

Mountains of Florida XX

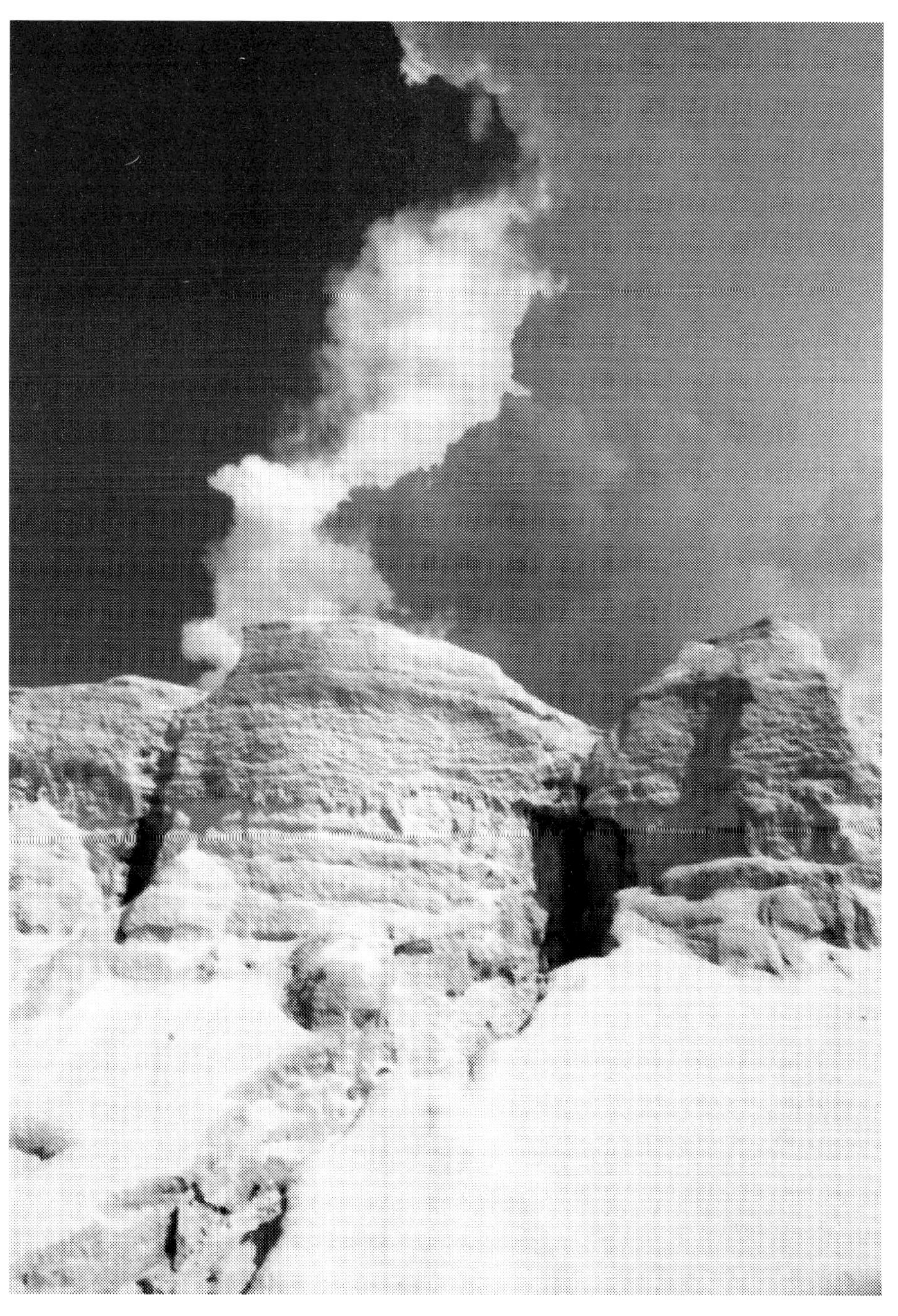

Mountains of Florida XXI

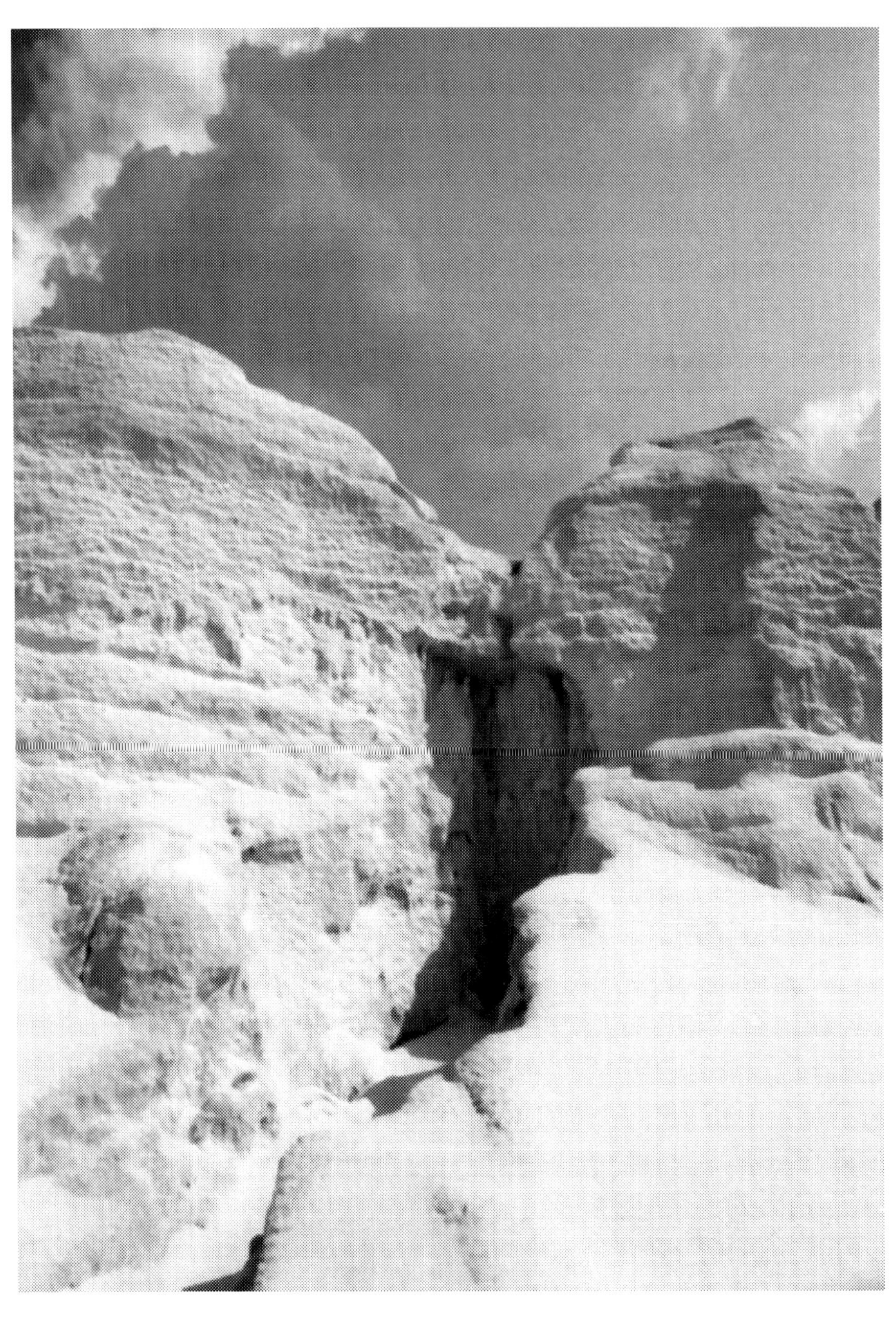

Mountains of Florida XXII

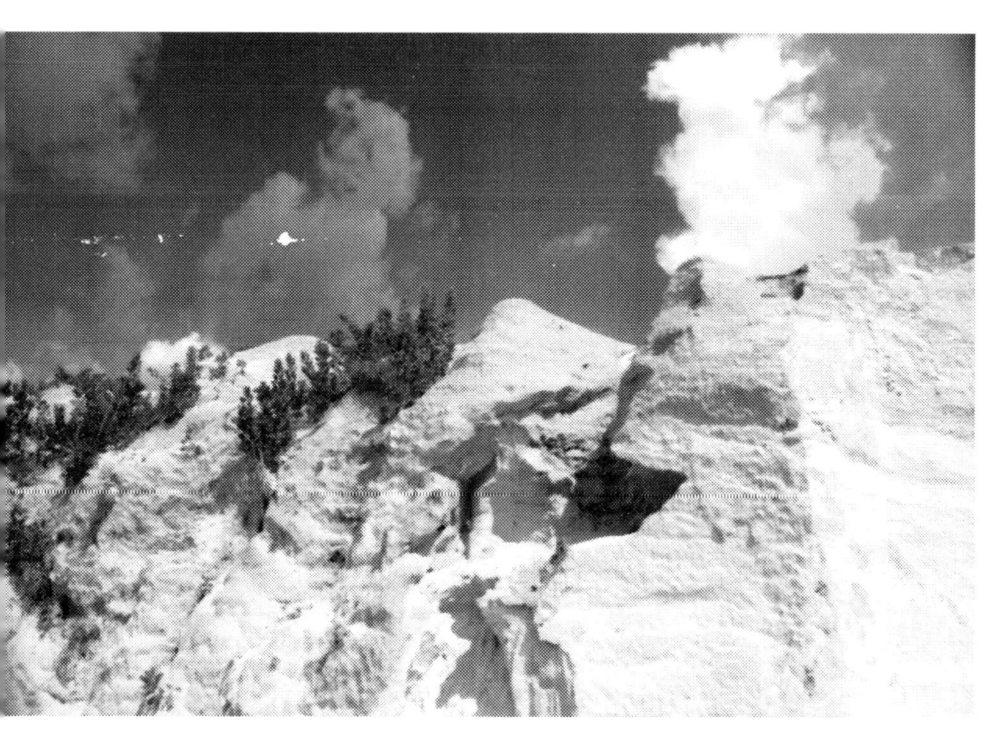

Mountains of Florida XXIII

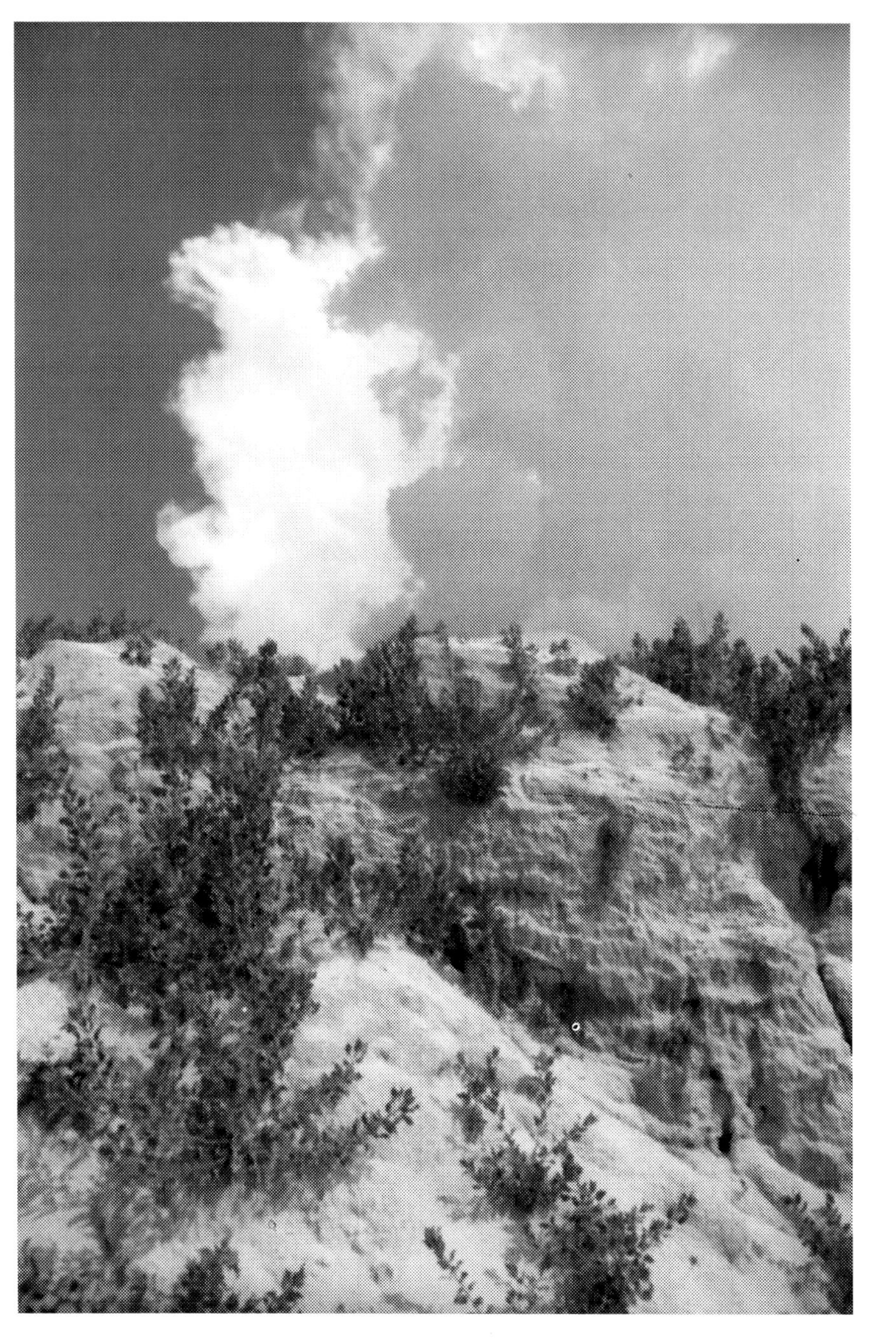

Mountains of Florida XXIV

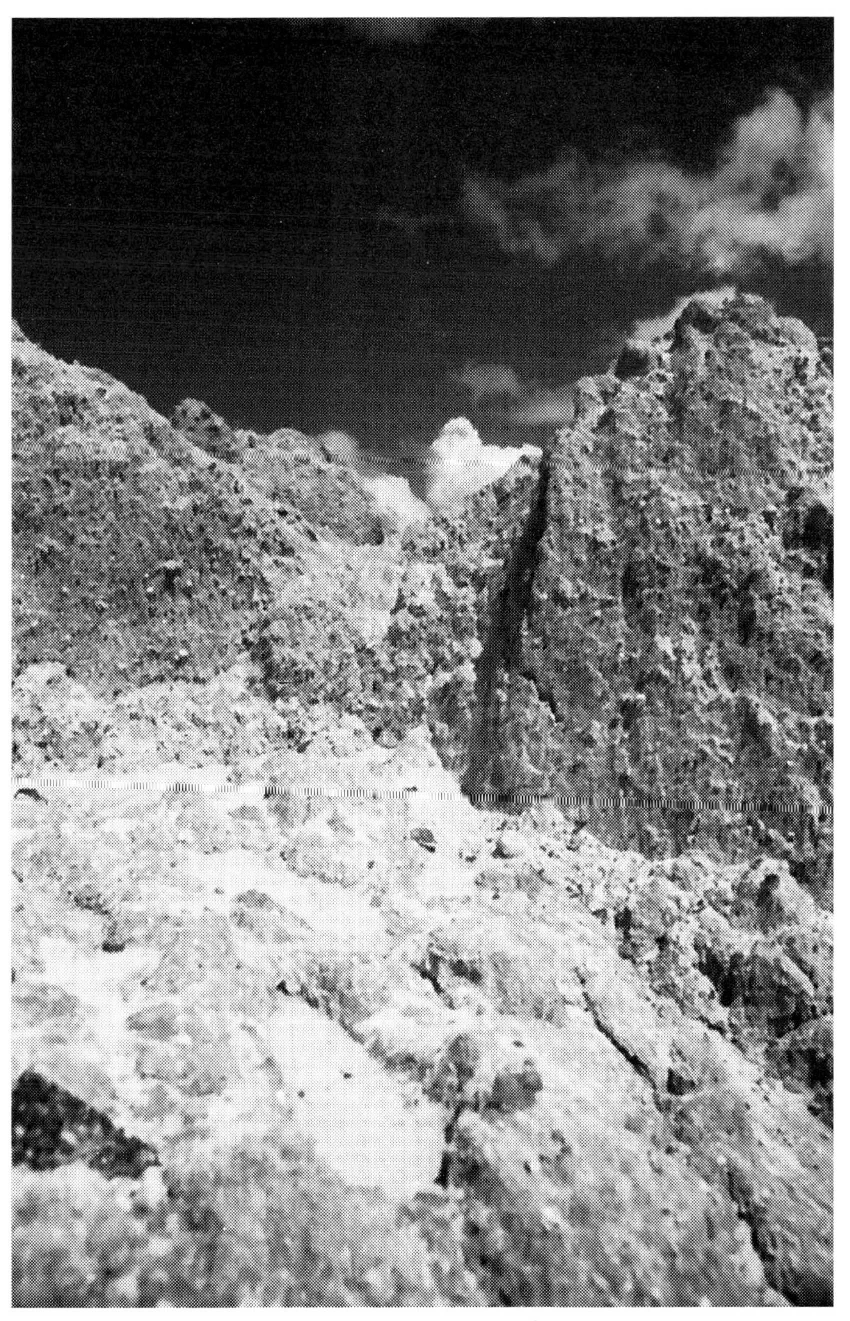

Mountains of Florida XXV

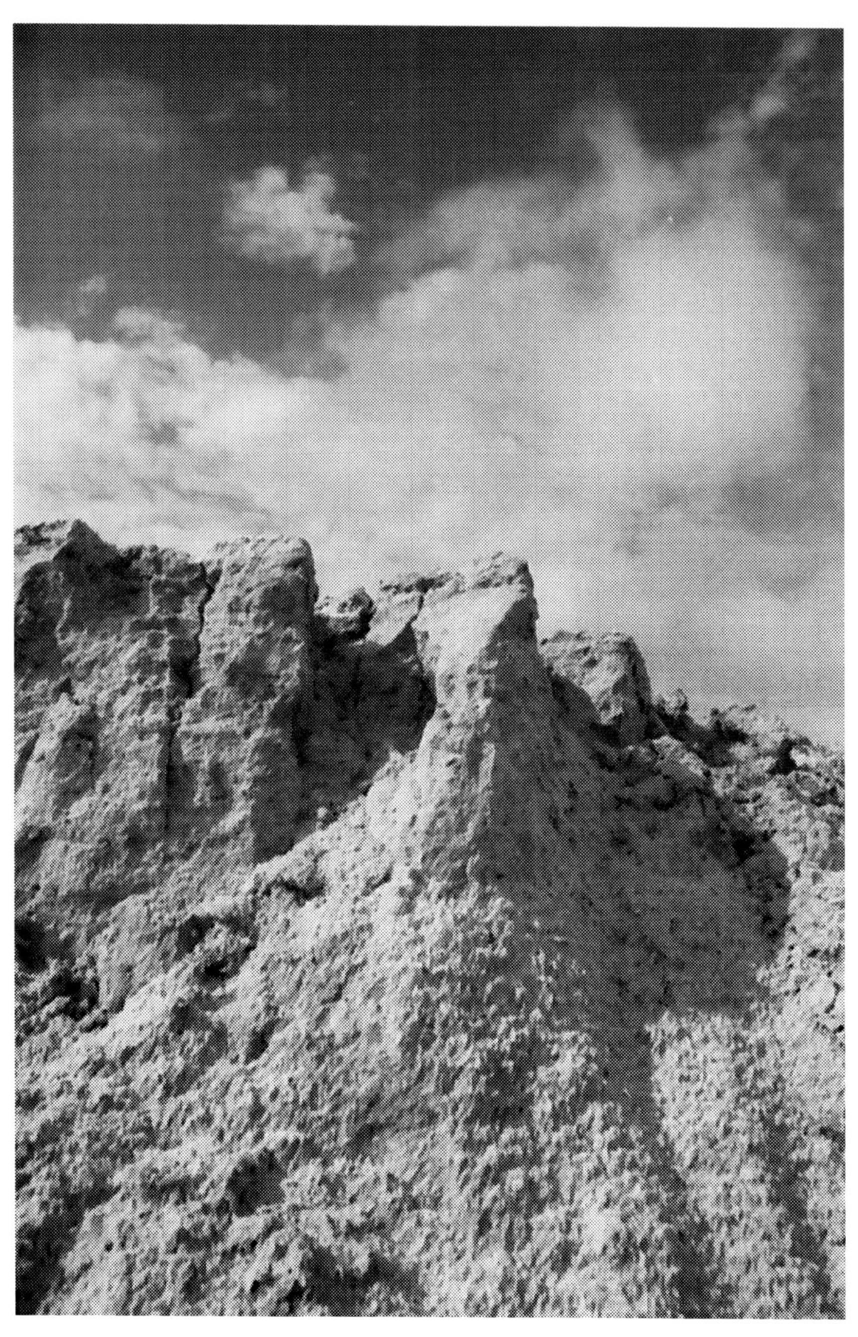

Mountains of Florida XXVI

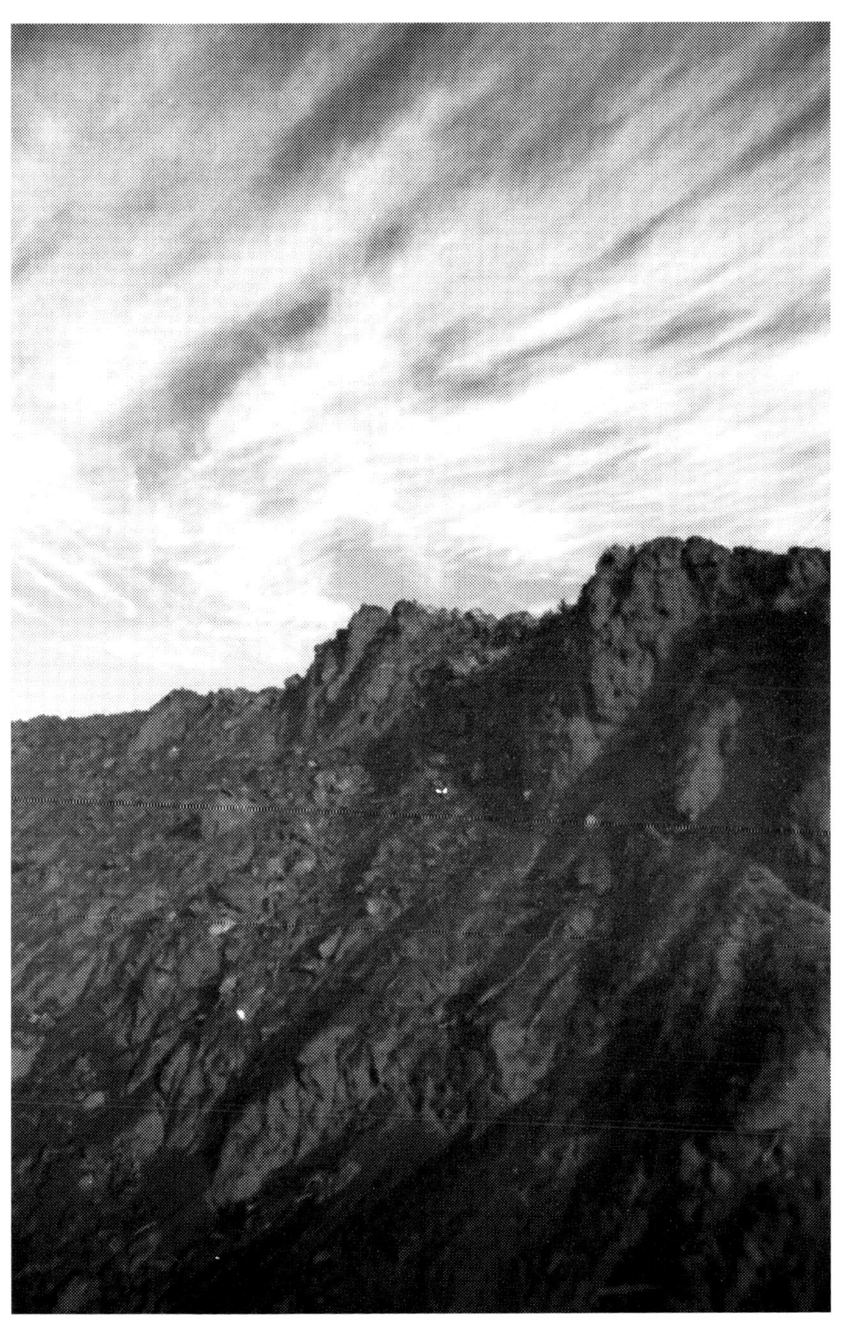

Mountains of Florida XXVII

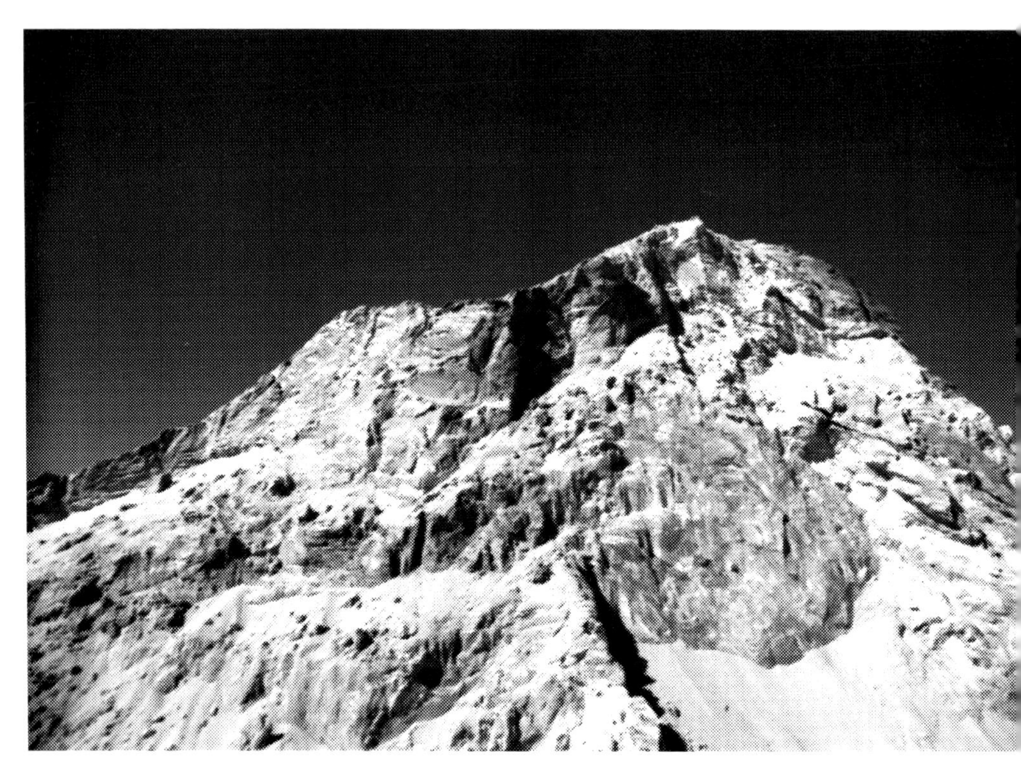

Mountains of Florida XXVIII

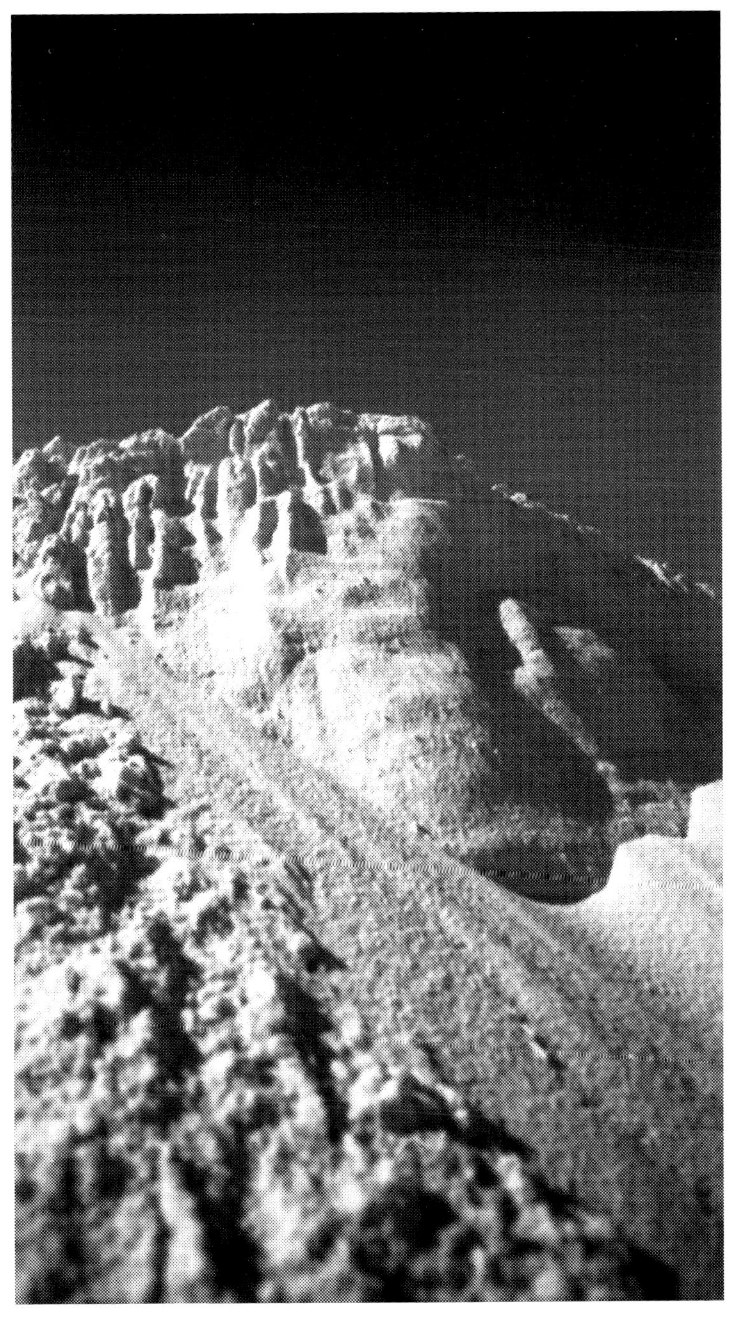

Mountains of Florida XXIX

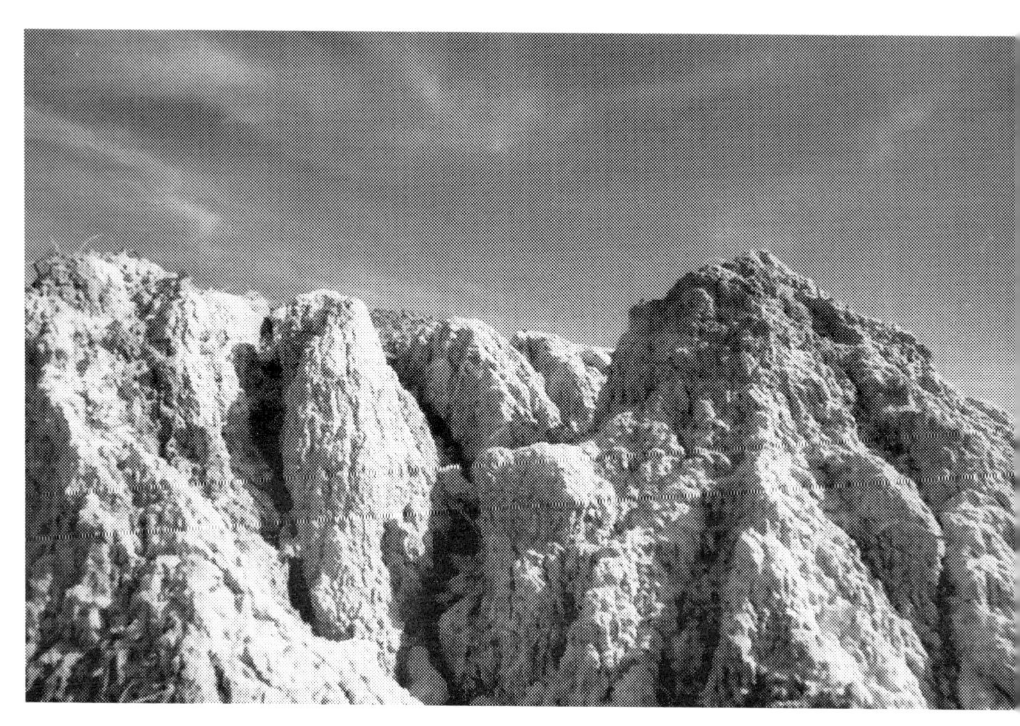

Mountains of Florida XXX

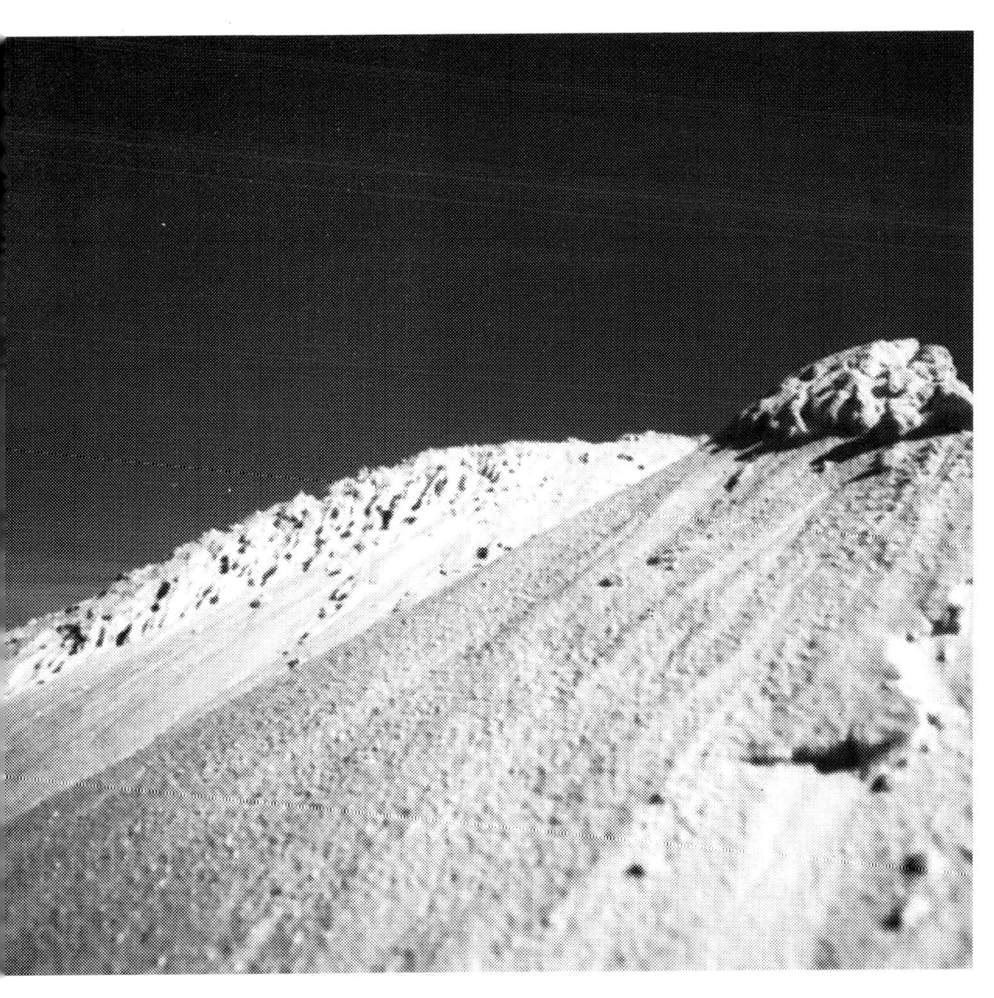

Mountains of Florida XXXI

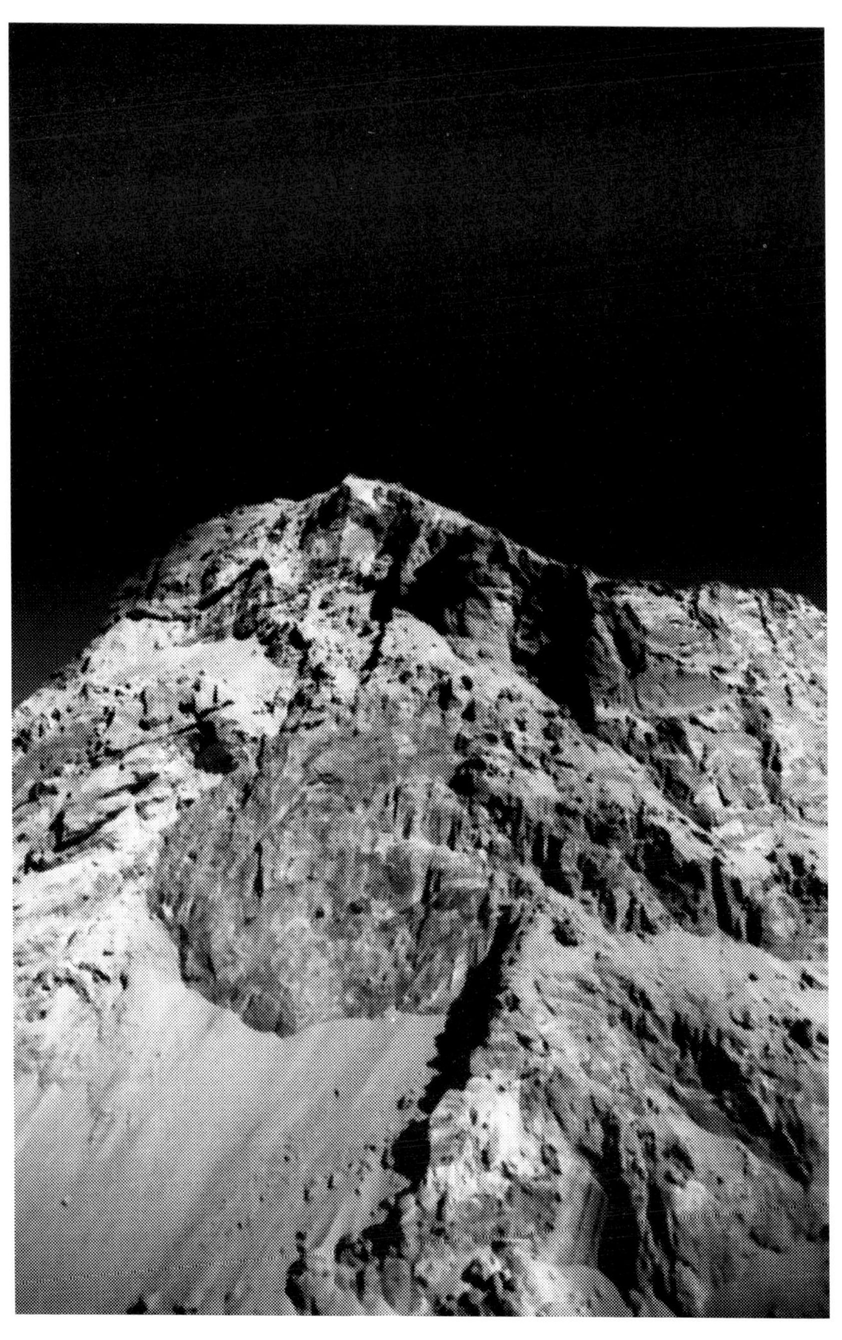

Mountains of Florida XXXII

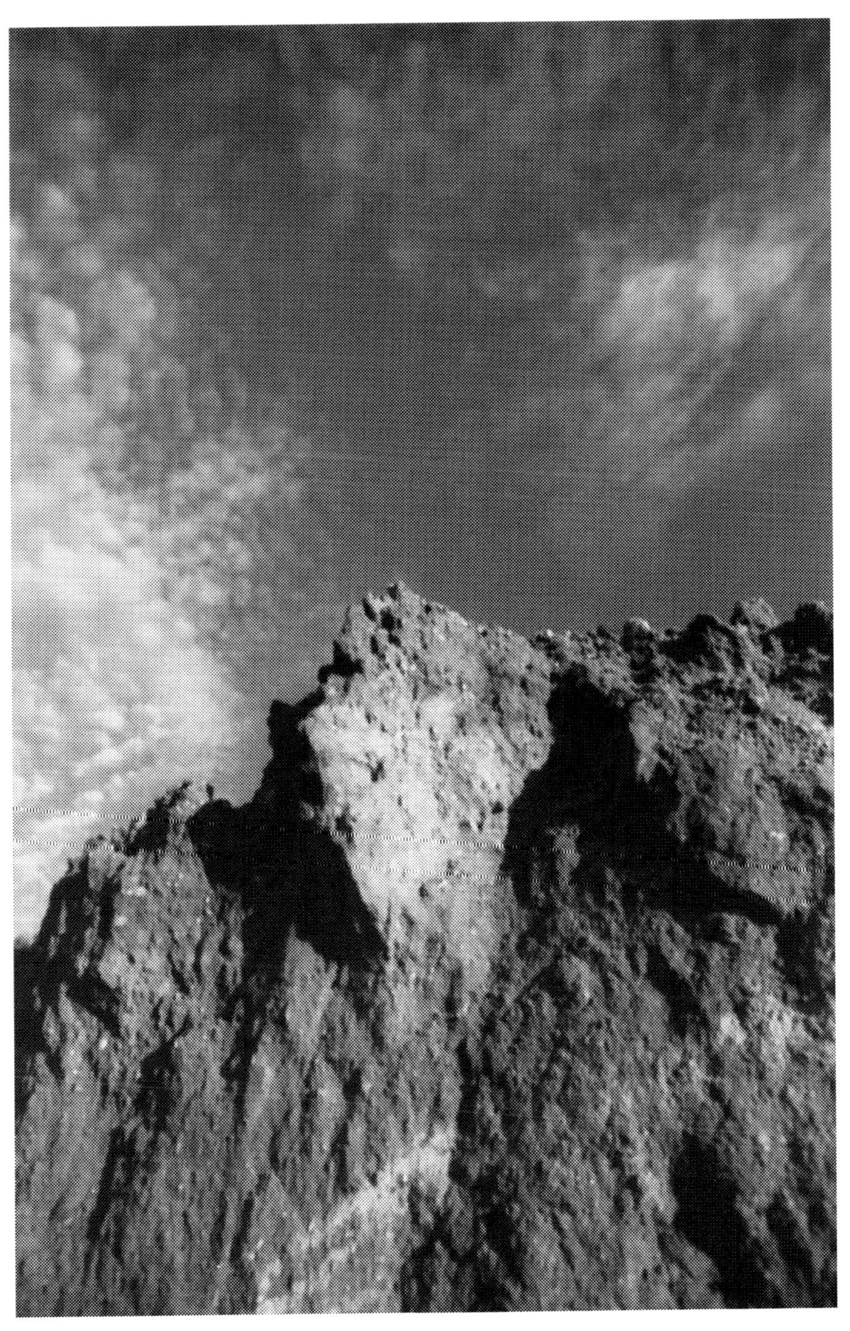

Mountains of Florida XXXIII

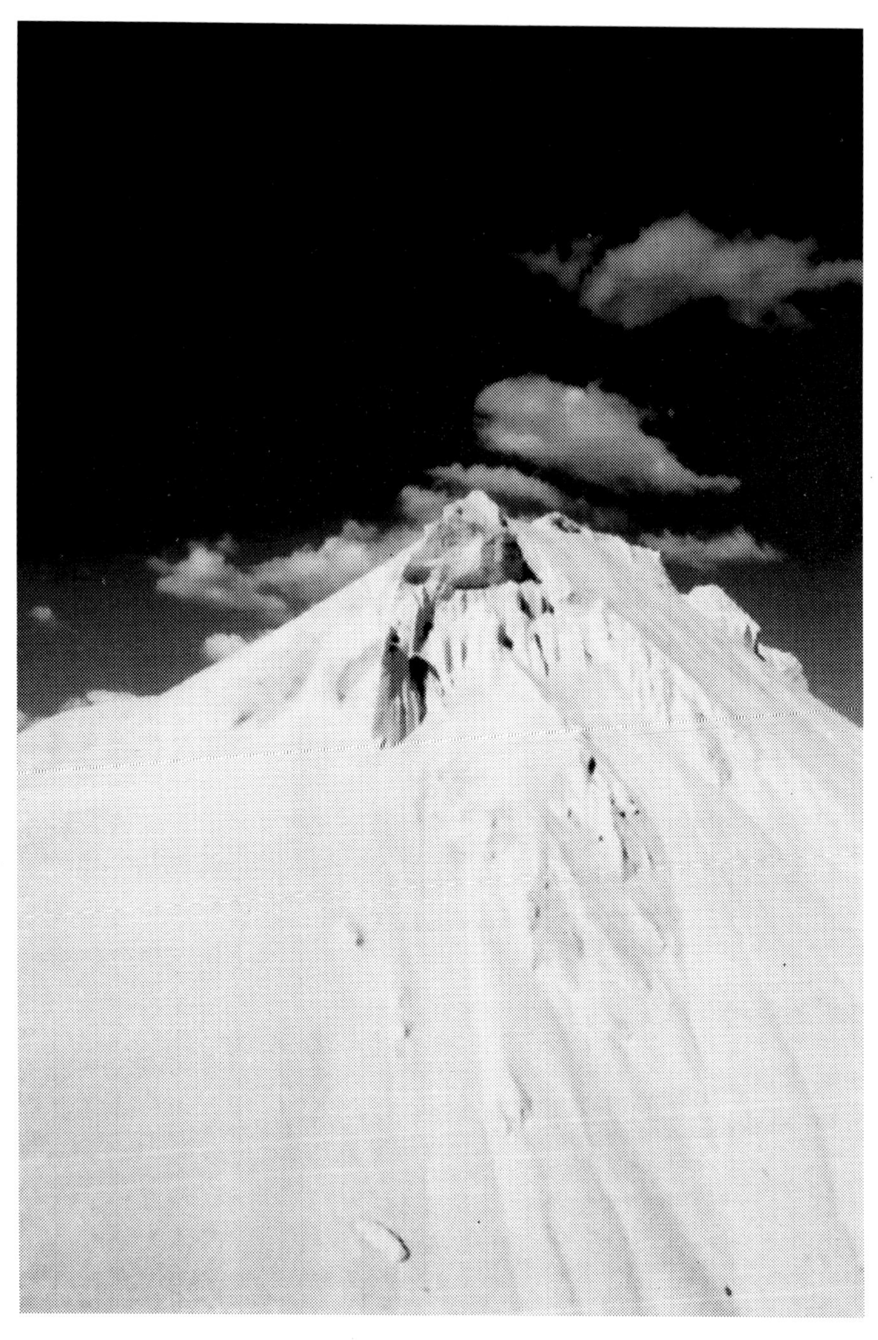

Mountains of Florida XXXIV

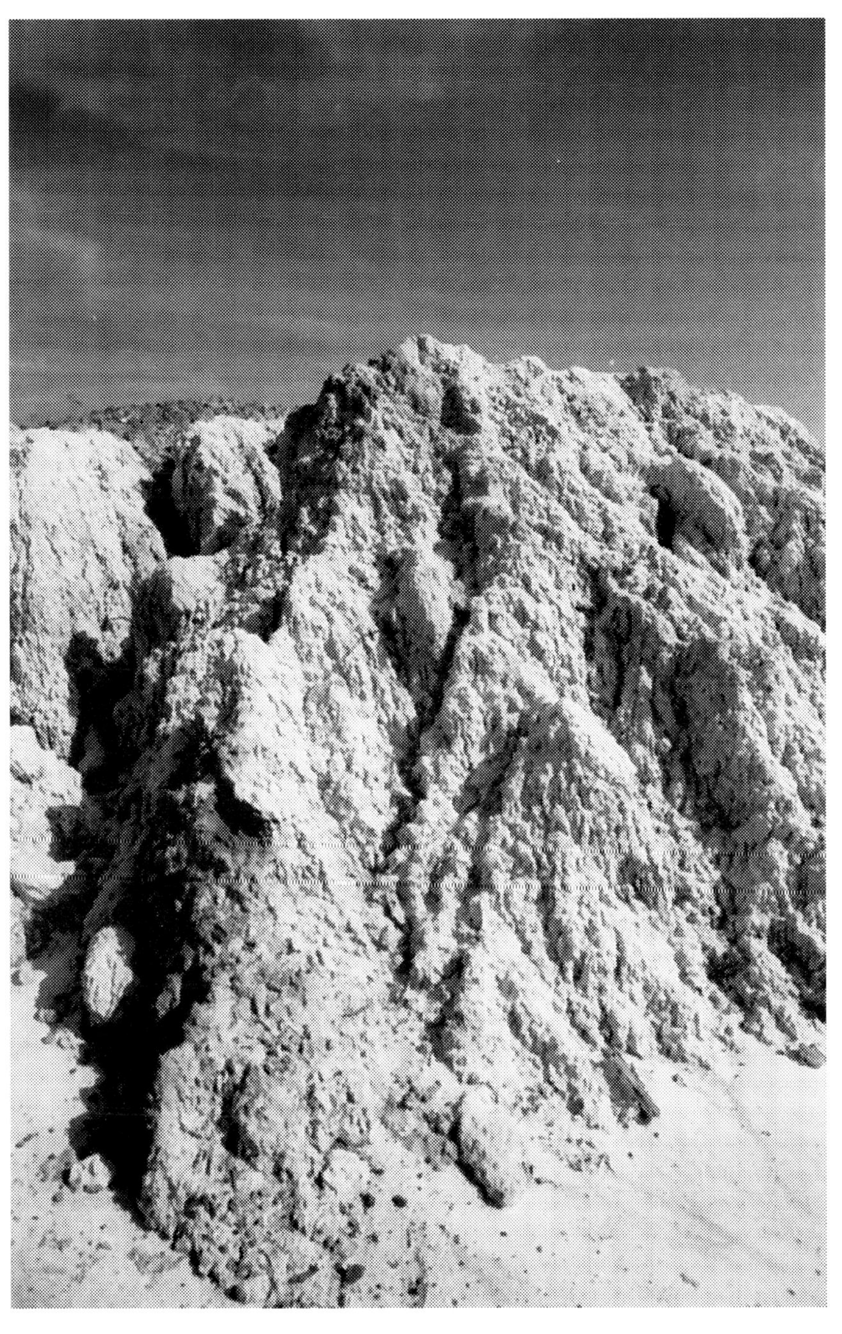

Mountains of Florida XXXV

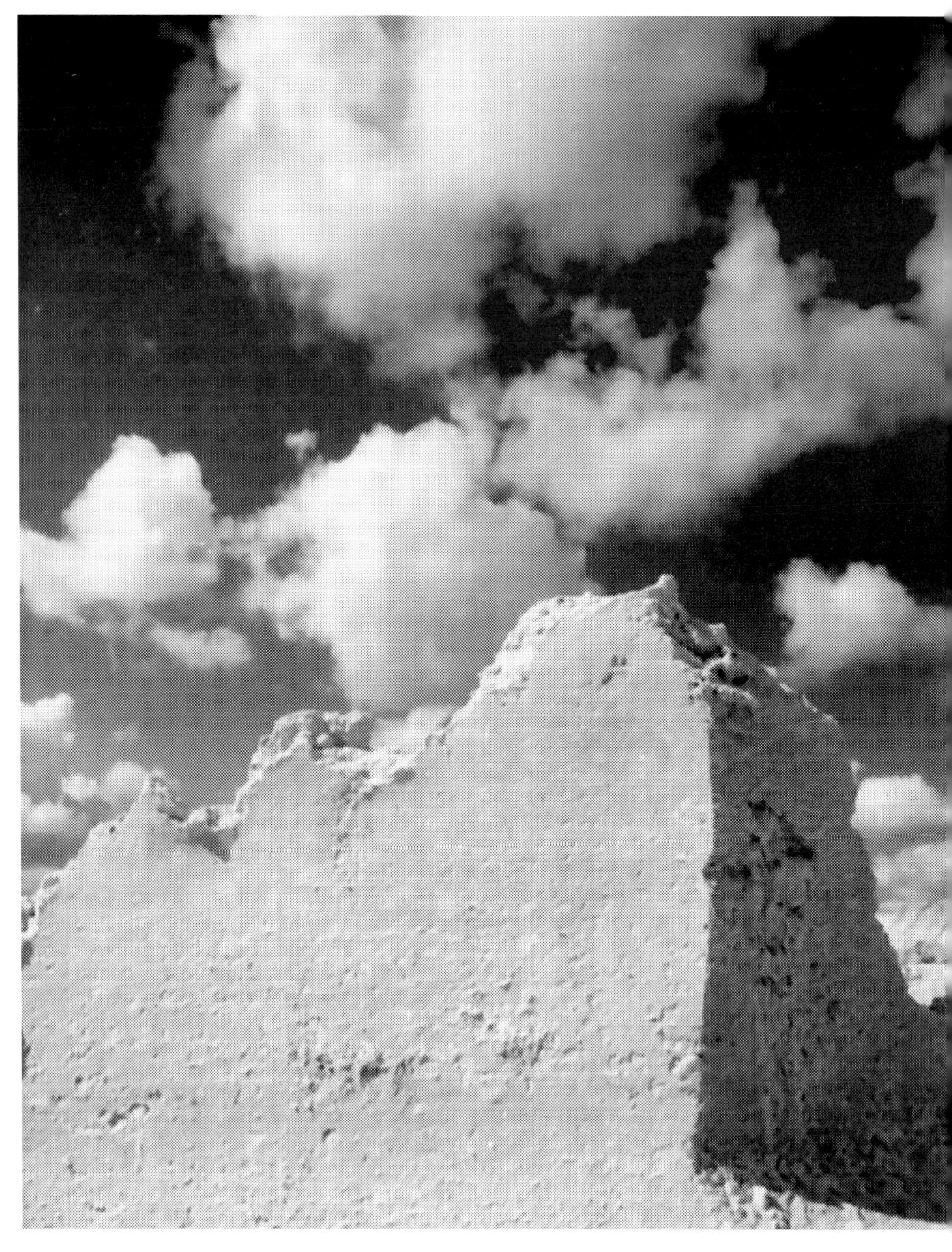

Mountains of Florida XXXVI

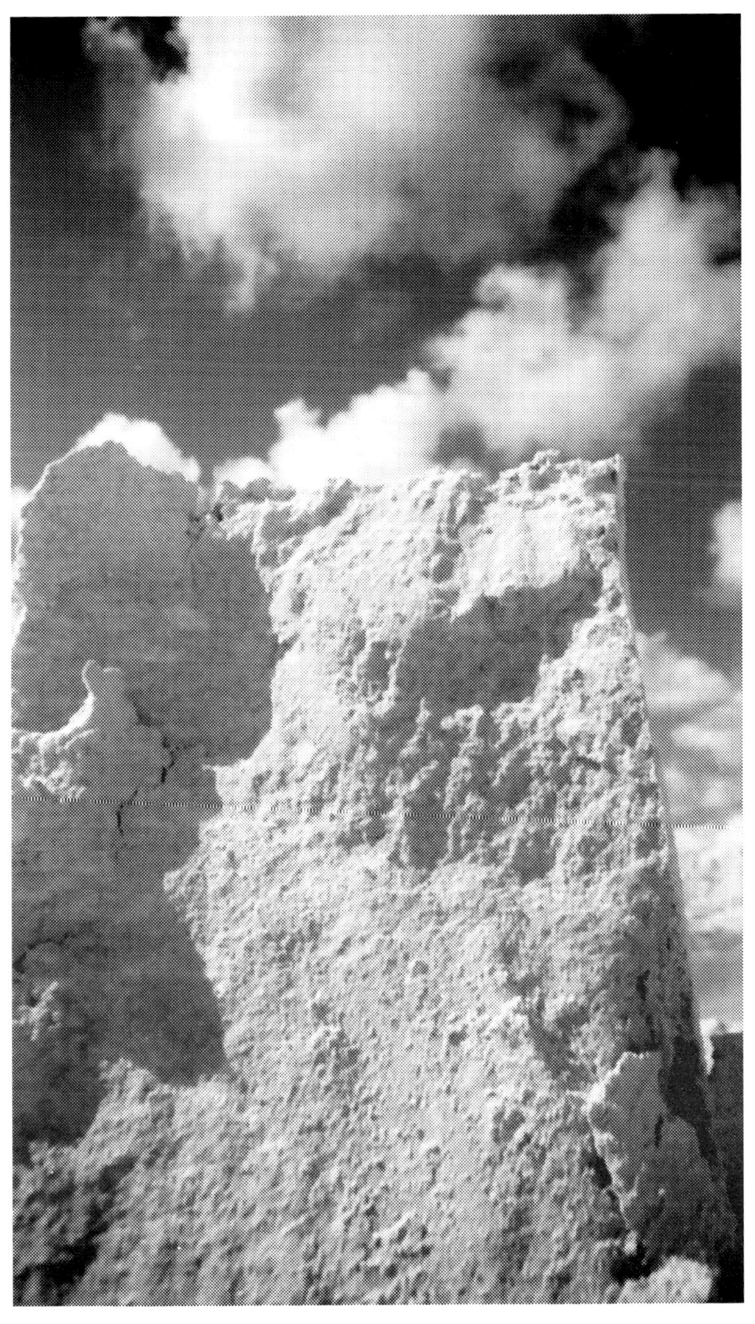

Mountains of Florida XXXVII

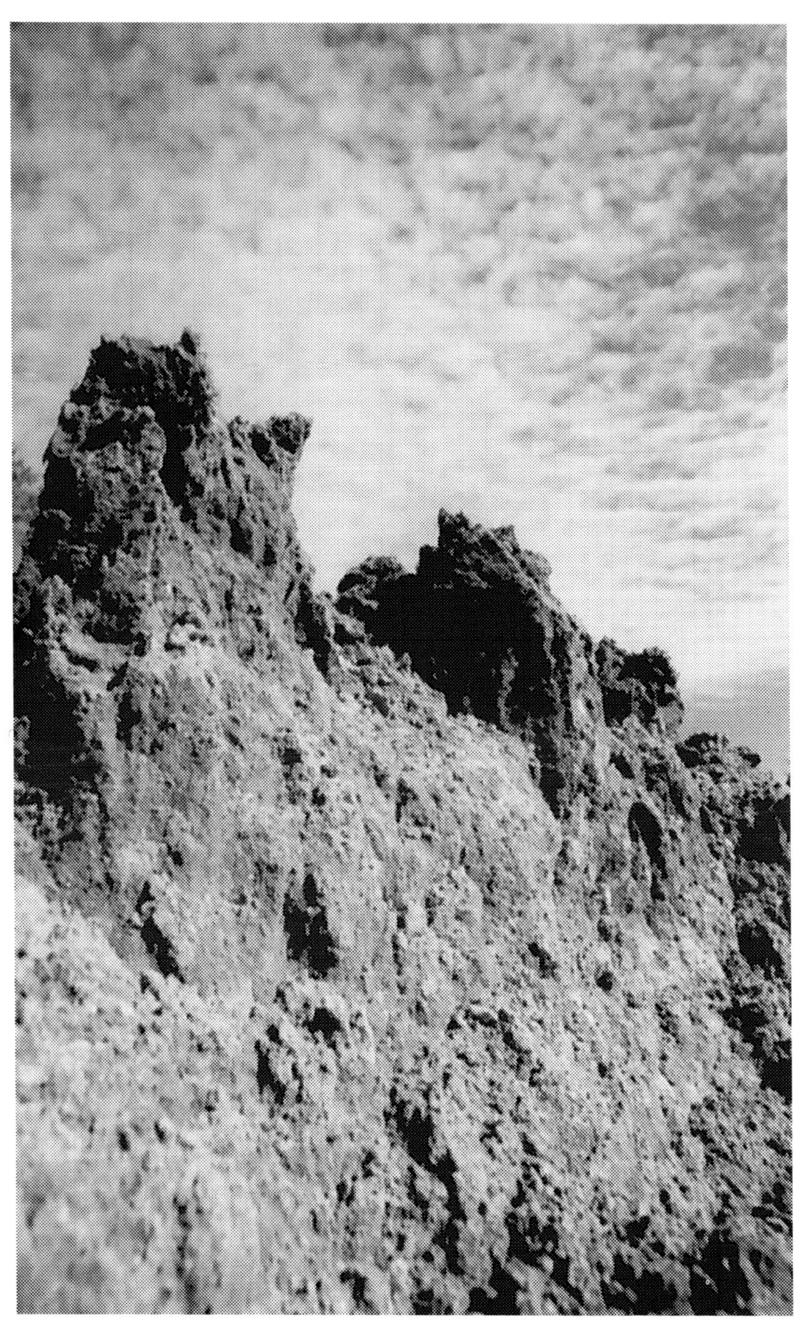

Mountains of Florida XXXVIII

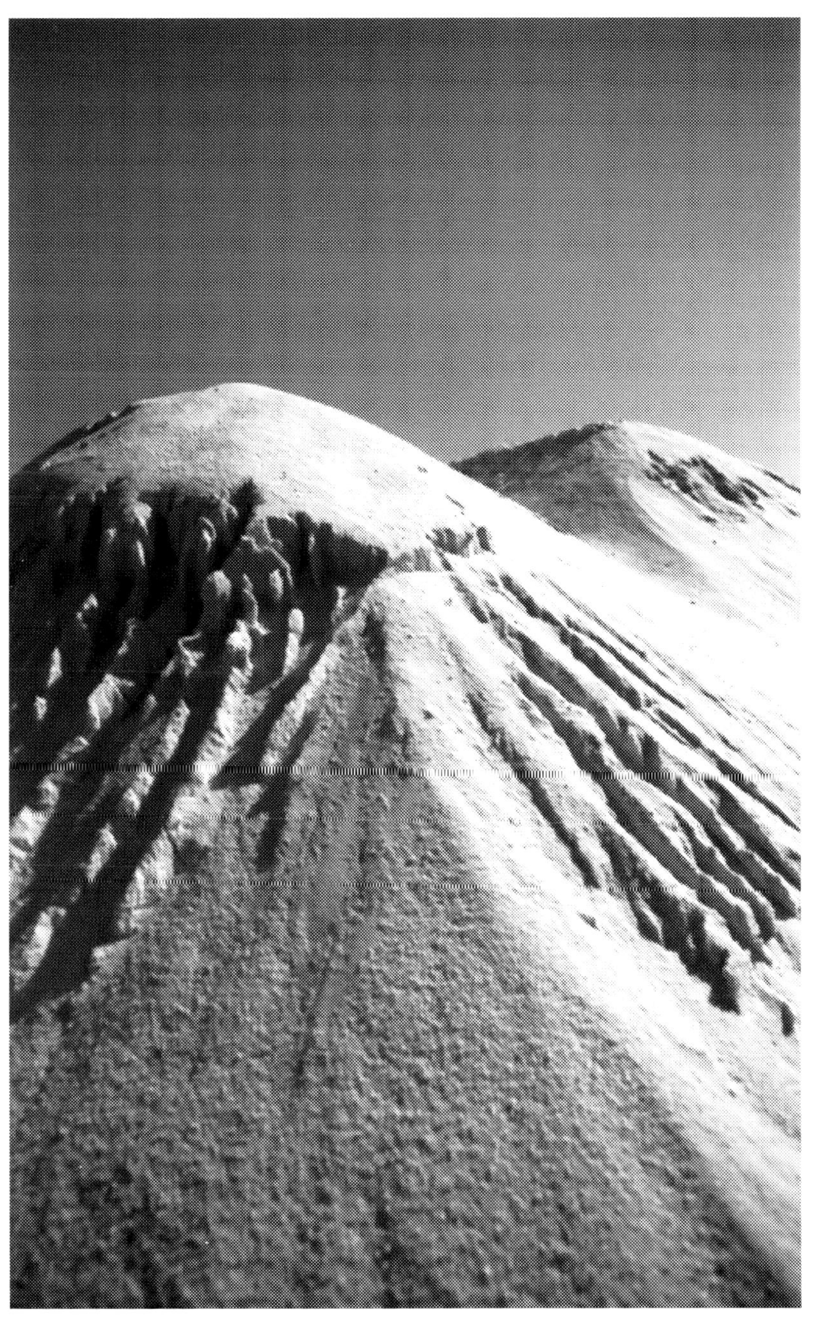

Mountains of Florida XXXIX

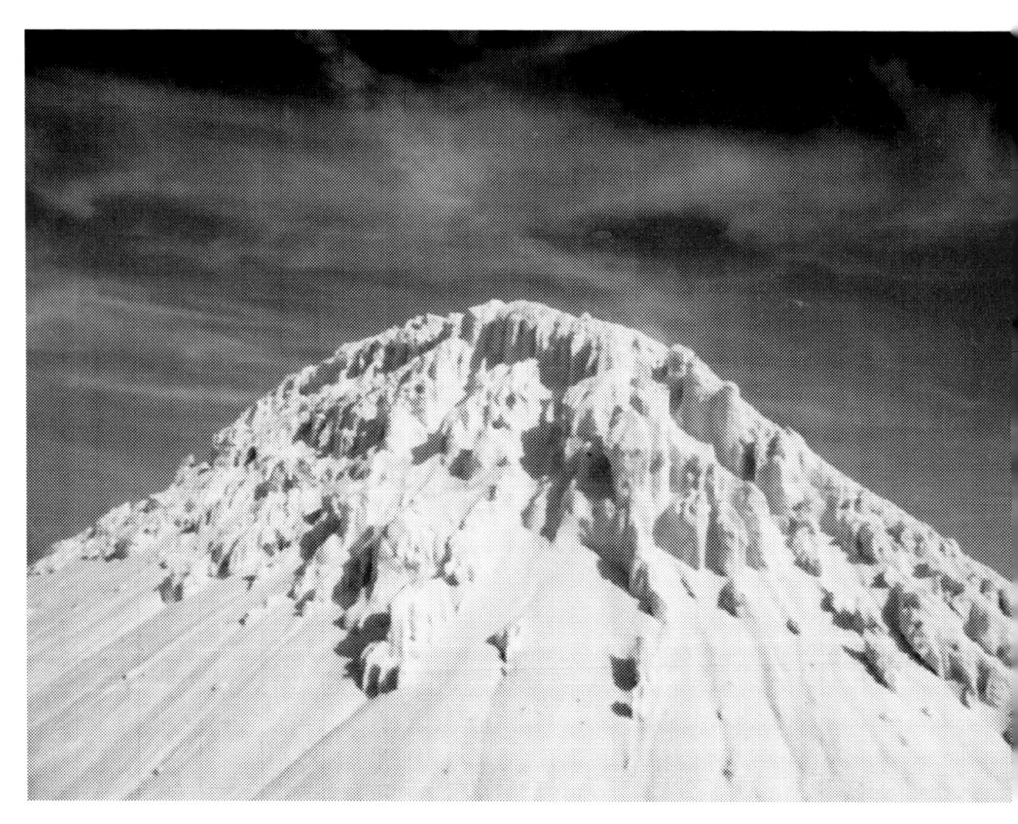

Mountains of Florida XL

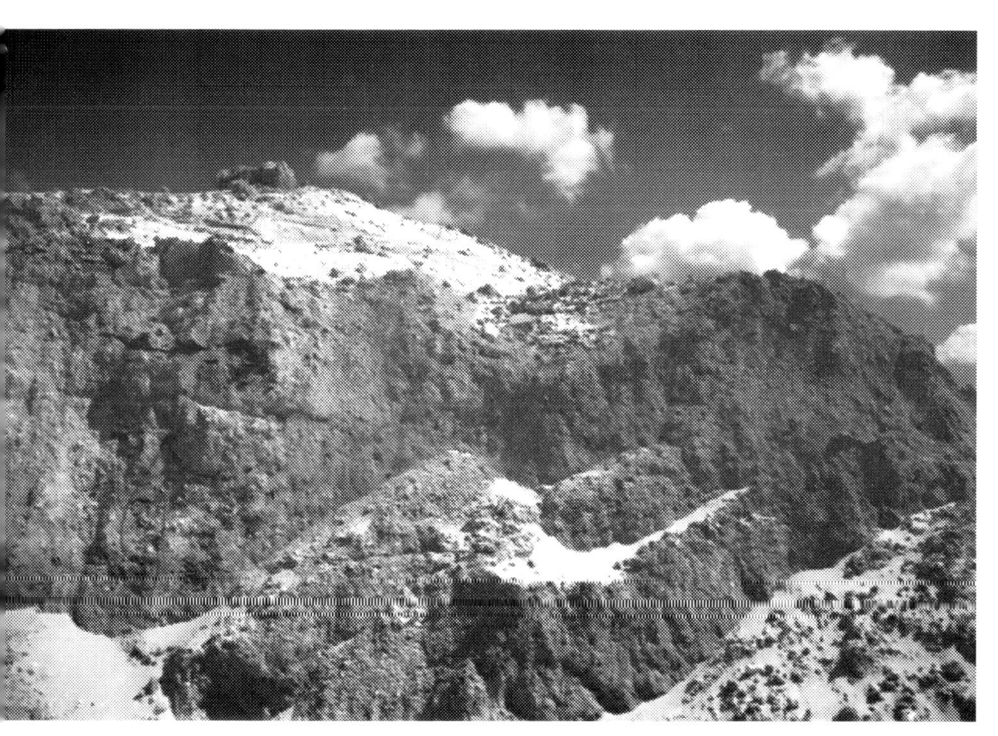

Mountains of Florida XLI

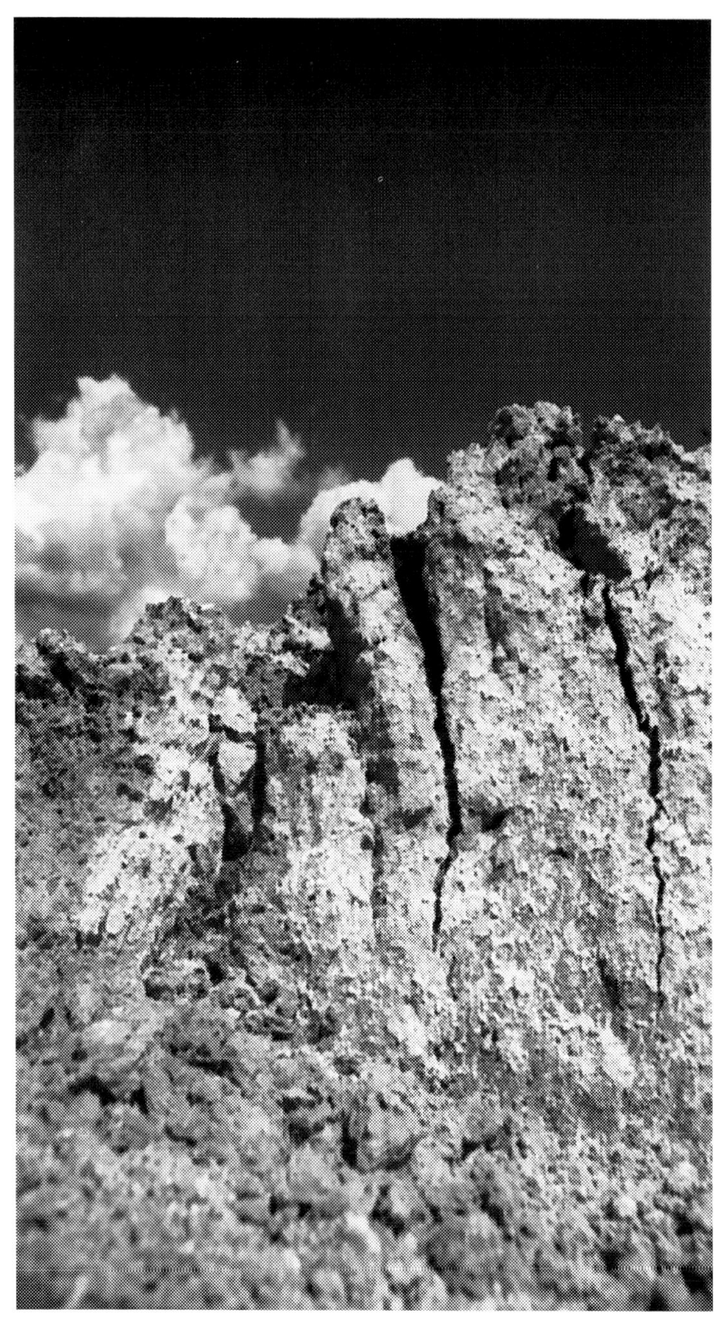

Mountains of Florida XLII

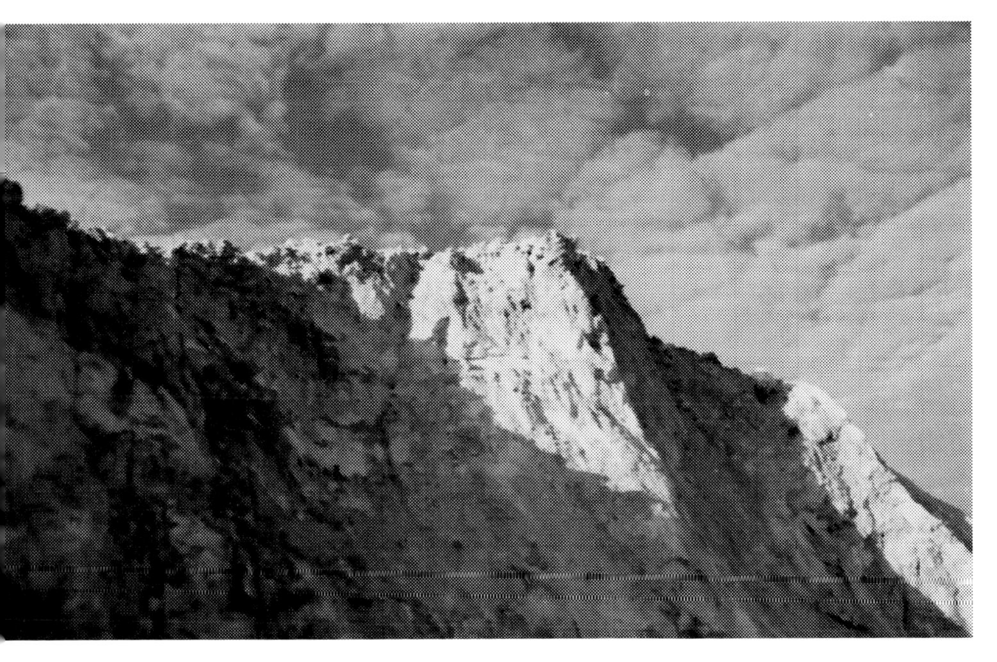

Mountains of Florida XLIII

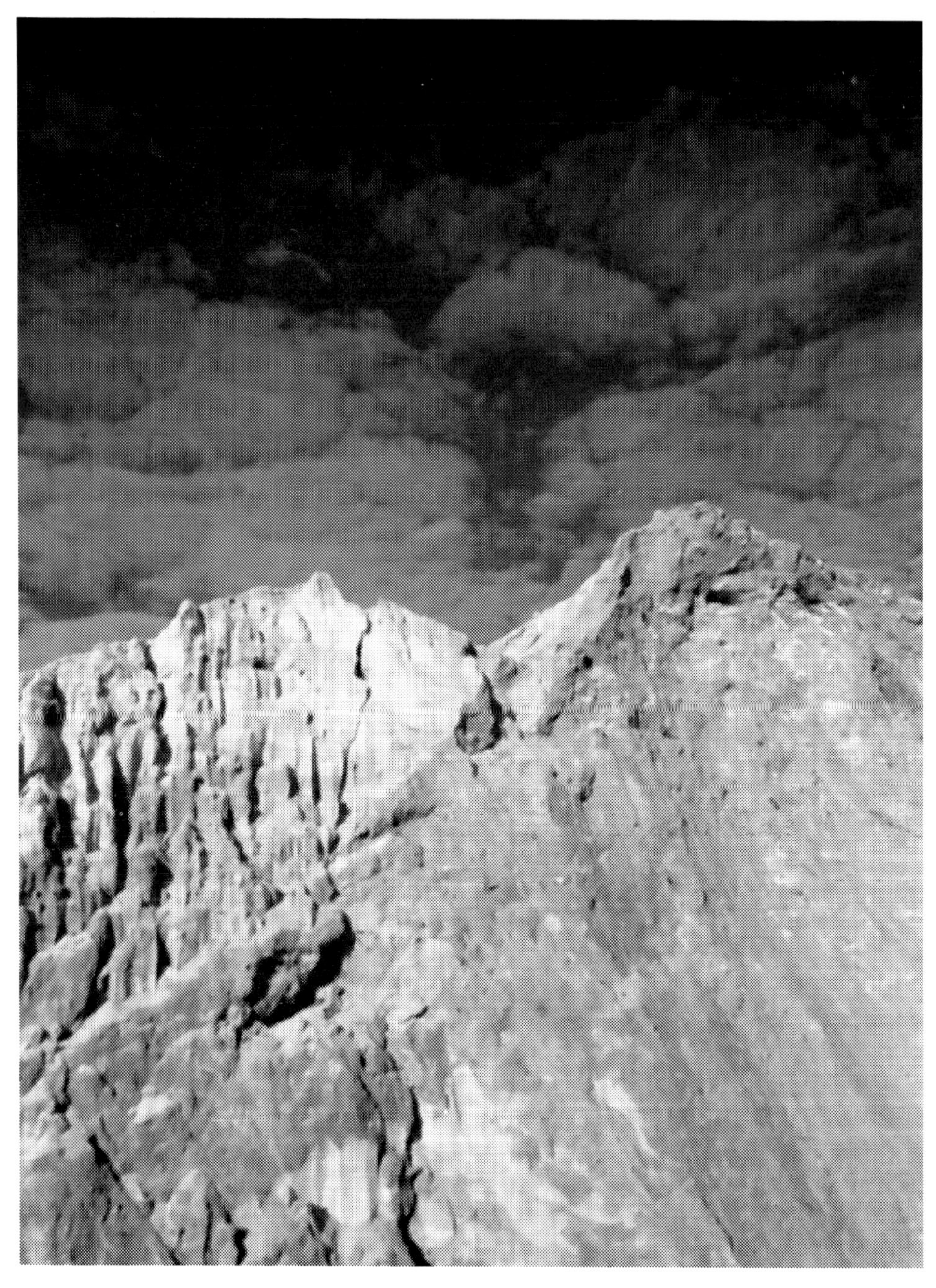

Mountains of Florida XLIV

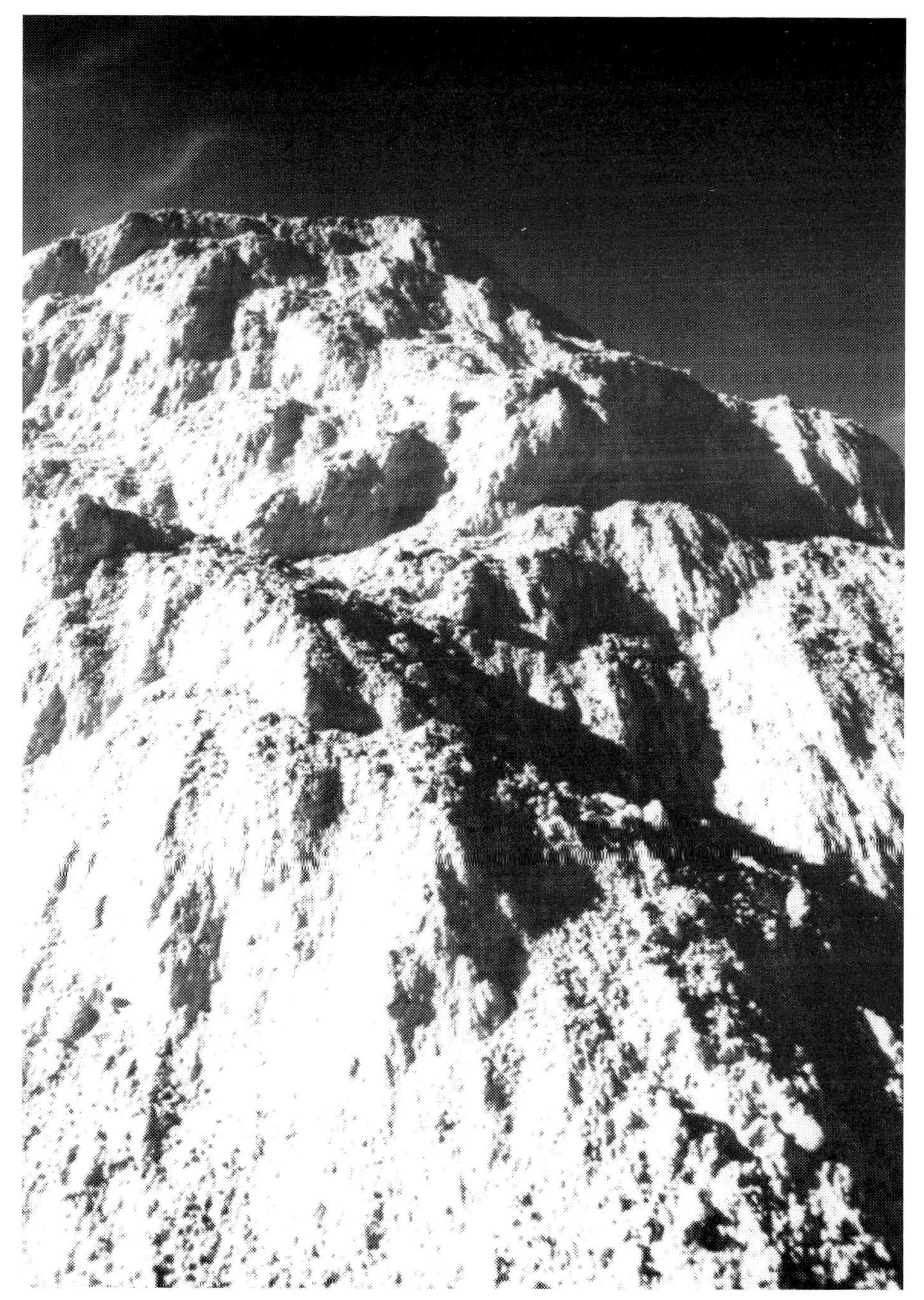

Mountains of Florida XLV

Roman Numeral Reference Table & Dirt Identification

1 I Spodic Dirt
2 II Spodic Dirt Sugar Sand
3 III Spodic Dirt Sugar Sand
4 IV Iron Ore Sugar Sand
5 V Spodic Dirt
6 VI Spodic Dirt
7 VII Iron Ore Spodic Dirt
8 VIII Iron Ore Sugar Sand
9 IX Mason Sand
10 X Spodic Dirt
11 XI Spodic Dirt
12 XII Iron Ore Sugar Sand
13 XIII Iron Ore Sugar Sand
14 XIV Spodic Dirt
15 XV Spodic Dirt
16 XVI Spodic Dirt
17 XVII Spodic Dirt
18 XVIII Iron Ore
19 XIX Iron Ore
20 XX Iron Ore
21 XXI Iron Ore Sugar Sand
22 XXII Iron Ore Sugar Sand
23 XXIII Iron Ore Scrub Brush
24 XXIV Iron Ore Scrub Brush
25 XXV Spodic Dirt
26 XXVI Spodic Dirt

27 XXVII Spodic Dirt
28 XXVIII Spodic Dirt
29 XXIX Mason Sand
30 XXX Spodic Dirt
31 XXXI Mason Sand
32 XXXII Spodic Dirt
33 XXXIII Spodic Dirt
34 XXXIV Mason Sand
35 XXXV Spodic Dirt
36 XXXVI Iron Ore
37 XXXVII Iron Ore
38 XXXVIII Spodic Dirt Sugar Sand
39 XXXIX Mason Sand
40 XL Mason Sand
41 XLI Spodic Dirt Sugar Sand
42 XLII Mason Sand
43 XLIII Spodic Dirt
44 XLIV Spodic Dirt
45 XLV Iron Ore